The MONOCLE
Travel Guide Series

Venice

All rights reserved. No part of this publication may be reproduced or transmitted in any form or by any means, electronic or mechanical, including photocopy or any storage and retrieval system, without permission in writing from the publisher.

Respect copyrights, encourage creativity!

For more information, please visit *gestalten.com*

Bibliographic information published by the Deutsche Nationalbibliothek: The Deutsche Nationalbibliothek lists this publication in the Deutsche Nationalbibliografie; detailed bibliographic data are available online at *dnb.d-nb.de*

This book was printed on paper certified by the FSC®

Monocle editor in chief and chairman: *Tyler Brûlé*
Monocle editor: *Andrew Tuck*
Books editor: *Joe Pickard*
Guide editor: *Chloë Ashby*

Designed by *Monocle*
Proofreading by *Monocle*
Typeset in *Plantin & Helvetica*

Printed by *Offsetdruckerei Grammlich, Pliezhausen*

Made in Germany

Published by *Gestalten*, Berlin 2017
ISBN 978-3-89955-903-3

© Die Gestalten Verlag GmbH & Co. KG, Berlin 2017

Welcome
—— Lagoon living

Venice's *watery location* makes it unique: no other city can claim to be made up of more than 100 islands threaded together by canals and bridges and supported by pieces of timber driven into mud. It's preposterous; it shouldn't work. Yet somehow, despite the odds, here it is.

Architecturally the city can feel like a historical collage, an amalgamation of visual imagery appropriated from neighbours east and west. But know where to look and you'll discover a smattering of contemporary structures by the likes of *Carlo Scarpa* that sharpen the otherwise frilly, palazzo-packed cityscape.

La Serenissima has long been a centre of *commerce*, *ingenuity* and *drive* (it's no coincidence that the Venetians invented the cheque) but as the tourists come marching in and the city adapts to their whims, quality and innovation can be a little harder to find.

This is where The Monocle Travel Guide to Venice steps in. We'll steer you safely past Piazza San Marco to the *independent businesses* making a mark on the shopping world and the design-savvy stop-ins shaking up the hotel scene. We've also got the scoop on where to head for the *freshest seafood* and the *tastiest cichèti*.

Venice is famously tricky to navigate: there's a notable *absence of wheels* (the only taxis and buses you'll see here have a port and starboard) so you're best off exploring on foot. Let us lead you away from the crowds and show you a different side to the lagoon city – naturally, with regular pit-stops at our favourite *bàcari* and perhaps a spritz or two. — (M)

Venice
Contents

Contents
— Navigating the city

Use the key below to help navigate the guide section by section.

 Hotels

 Food and drink

 Retail

 Things we'd buy

Essays

Culture

Design and architecture

Sport and fitness

Best of the rest

 Walks

012 — 013
Map
Explore Venice with our handy map, helping you get to grips with the key areas covered in this guide.

014 — 015
Need to know
From *acqua alta* to the Venetian dialect, here are some of the basics for navigating the city's streets and sights.

016 — 025
Hotels
When it comes to accommodation Venice has gilded palazzos aplenty – but there's also a clutch of cutting-edge apartments and tranquil canal-side B&Bs. Get up to speed on where to stay for business or pleasure with our guide to the best hotels.

026 — 045
Food and drink
Don't expect to find pages packed with lasagne and pizza. We head off the bustling *campi* and into the jumbled backstreets to discover the trattorias serving the freshest seafood and the best *bàcari* for a cheeky spritz.

026 — 031
Restaurants

031 — 035
Bàcari

036 — 038
Lunch

038 — 039
Sweet treats

040 — 042
Coffee

042 — 045
Drinks

046 — 061
Retail
From traditional tailoring to model boats, Venice has kept its age-old ateliers alive amid today's shiny boutiques. Dodge the souvenir shops and discover the retailers worth visiting with our pick of independent businesses that are both forging their own identity and reinterpreting age-old crafts.

046 — 048
Menswear

048 — 050
Womenswear

050 — 051
Mixed fashion

052 — 053
Homeware

054 — 059
Specialist retail

060
Opticians

060 — 061
Bookshops

062 — 064
Things we'd buy
Forget tacky, sequined trinkets: here's our guide to the essential take-homes for visitors.

065 — 088
Essays
Venice can be as tricky to get to grips with as the city centre's contorted *calli*. Monocle family and friends straighten out the kinks, helping to paint a picture of what life here is really like.

010

Venice
Contents

089 — 103
Culture
We steer you through the city's ever-evolving art scene, from renaissance masterpieces to modern marvels. Plus: old and new libraries, grand theatres, a Venetian master's workshop and everything in between.

089 — 096
Museums and galleries

097 — 099
Commercial galleries

100 — 101
Libraries and workshops

101 — 103
Live venues

103
Media round-up

104 — 121
Design and architecture
Venice is crammed with classical churches and palazzos but know where to look and you'll soon discover many surprising modernist twists. From Carlo Scarpa's 20th-century creations to the international pavilions of the biennale, we select our best-loved buildings and more.

104 — 106
Contemporary

106 — 109
Carlo Scarpa

110 — 112
20th century

113 — 115
Essential classics

115 — 117
Churches

118
Pavilions

119 — 121
Visual identity

122 — 125
Sport and fitness
Some say walking up and down Venice's umpteen bridges is exercise enough but if you really want to raise your heartbeat, here's a selection of places to work out. Plus, and perhaps more importantly, ways to wind down.

122 — 123
In and on the water

124
Grooming

124
Spas

125
Running routes

126 — 129
Best of the rest
The bars, basilicas and beaches to visit when you need a break from the crowds. Join us for a tour of the idyllic islands around the Venetian lagoon.

130 — 137
Walks
With its lack of wheels, Venice is made for walking and wherever you are you'll enjoy a different view. We map out picturesque walking routes around three of our favourite *sestieri*, as well as a quiet island a short vaporetto ride away.

130 — 131
Castello

132 — 133
Cannaregio

134 — 135
Dorsoduro

136 — 137
Giudecca

138 — 139
Resources
Be in the know with our bite-size guide to events, slang and the city's soundtrack, plus suggestions for what to do on a rainy day.

140 — 141
About Monocle
Find out more about our global brand from groundbreaking print, radio, online and film output through to our cafés and shops.

142 — 143
Acknowledgements
The people who put this guide together: writers, photographers, researchers and all the rest.

144 — 145
Index

Venice Map

Map
—— Canal-side cartography

Located in the Venetian lagoon on the edge of the Adriatic Sea, Venice was founded on a collection of 118 small islands in the 6th century by inhabitants of northeast Italy who were forced to flee by barbarian invasions. Over time the scattered settlements came together and public buildings were constructed to shore up the community.

By the 13th century the archipelago was organised in a unique urban system, divided into six neighbourhoods known as *sestieri*. The Canal Grande flows straight through the middle, splitting the six into two groups of three.

Each *sestiere* has a distinct personality. San Marco is always teeming with tourists, while charming Cannaregio offers a quiet snapshot of real life in the city. Castello is the biggest and greenest of the districts, San Polo is small but lively and bohemian Dorsoduro attracts a combination of culture vultures and students. And Santa Croce? It's home to the bus station, so it's where you bid farewell to wheels.

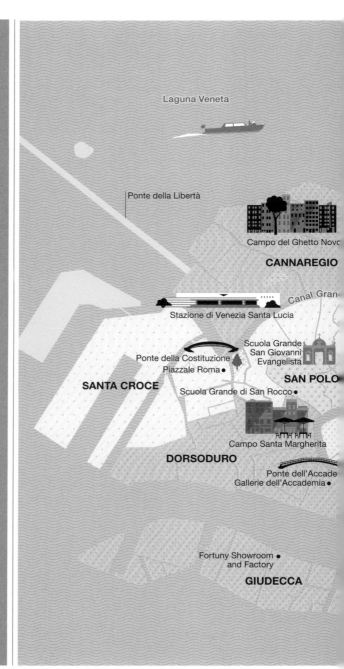

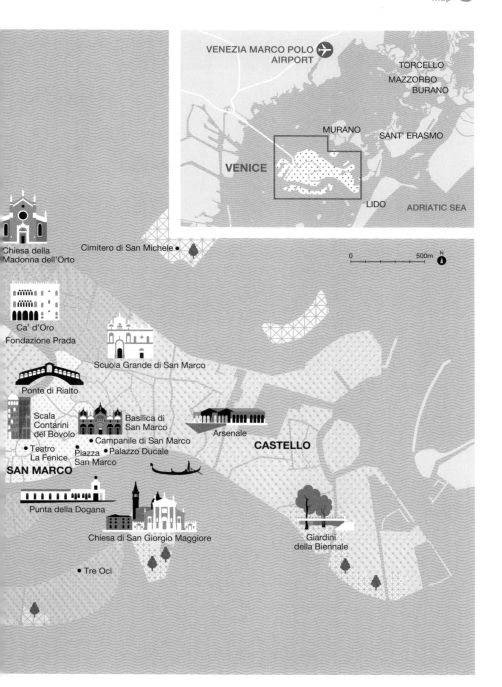

Venice — Need to know

Need to know
—— Get to grips with the basics

How to walk like a Venetian, navigate your way through the city's chaotic streets, dress for the occasion and enjoy a well-earned drink. Read on for our top tips and quick facts for visitors to Venice.

Etiquette
First impressions

Ciao may be the Italian word you feel most confident using but only do so when greeting someone you know; if you're meeting someone for the first time, stick to *buongiorno* (good morning) or *buonasera* (good evening). Friends often engage in a double kiss, usually first on the left cheek and then on the right, while new acquaintances shake hands and smile. It's also helpful to master some basics: *per favore* (please), *grazie* (thank you) and *parla inglese?* (do you speak English?).

Walking
Pointers for pedestrians

Venice is a car-free city – and no wonder, with its framework of waterways and tiny streets. The best way to explore is definitely by foot. Just try to remember the following do's and don'ts.

Freestyle can be tricky. By all means mosey through the piazzas and along the waterfronts but stick to the right-hand side in the city centre's skinny streets, falling into single file if necessary.

Similarly, take care not to block bridges. If you want to take a photograph, move aside so you don't cause a human traffic jam. And whatever you do, don't plump for a bridge when it comes to tucking into your panino: other than irritating passers-by you may end up being moved. Picnicking in public is frowned upon and in some places supposedly even banned. Having said that, find a quieter spot and you should be fine.

I just don't recognise myself anymore

Seasons
Cold comfort

Whenever you visit there are going to be tourists but in the bitterly cold winter months the streets are quieter and the hordes fewer and further between. The calm extends through to April – forgetting February, which is always heaving with Carnevale – when wisteria shows the first signs of spring. May is possibly the best time to visit the city.

In summer both the heat and the number of visitors rise, while the locals escape for their holidays. If you can avoid August, do: as well as tourists, the city is rife with mosquitoes.

Opening hours
All in the timing

The best restaurants are closed on Sundays and Mondays as the markets aren't open, meaning no fresh produce. Museums often close on either Mondays or Tuesdays (check individual websites). As well as Sundays, most boutiques and gift shops close on Monday mornings, while food shops can shut on Wednesday afternoons; hours tend to run from 09.00 to 19.30, with lunch and a nap between 13.00 and 16.00.

Venice
Need to know

Tipping
At your service

There are no set rules. All restaurants charge a *coperto* (cover charge), usually €2 or €3 a head, for sitting down and using the dishes and tablecloth; eat or drink standing at the bar and this doesn't apply. This goes to the owner rather than the waiter or waitress, so if you want to add a separate tip leave up to 10 per cent in cash. If the bill includes an additional charge called *servizio*, which is also about 10 per cent, this *is* the tip so no need to add extra.

Drinking
Raise a glass

Venice will never be short of water and you can happily drink it from a tap. If you're out you're also bound to bump into one of the city's 122 fountains before you run dry.

Spritz is the classic choice when you're craving something stronger and Venetians sip this glowing drink from as early as 11.00. Like most Italians, they enjoy their alcohol with a bite to eat. Wine is often simple and inexpensive, and can be ordered by the half-bottle and glass. Don't worry if you don't recognise the label: the best wineries don't advertise.

Come and join me for a spritz!

Acqua alta
Water cycle

You may have heard about *acqua alta* (high water): people still talk about 1966, when the city was submerged in almost two metres of salty water. But when and why does this periodic flooding occur? The contributing factors are a high tide, a low atmospheric pressure and a sirocco, a warm wind blowing water from the Adriatic Sea into the lagoon. This clash usually occurs from mid-October to the start of December and, when it does, high tide only lasts for a few hours. So don't let it dampen your trip; dive into a bar and wait it out.

Please can you pass the shampoo?

Clothing
Dress to impress

It's important to wear appropriate clothing when visiting certain churches and monuments, which basically means no bare arms and legs. Remember this is Venice, not Venice Beach. Swimming is not allowed in the canals, nor is walking around the city in a swimming costume or with a bare chest. The beaches on Lido are the only exception.

Addresses
Grey areas

The main island, which measures about 7 sq km, is sliced into six neighbourhoods known as *sestieri* (literally "sixths"), which you'll find on our map (*see page 12*). Woven in and out of these, however, is a complex web of streets.

Knowing the name of the street you're looking for isn't enough. These are often merely descriptive: singling out Calle Drio la Chiesa (Street Behind the Church), for example, isn't easy. To find an address you'll also need the name of the *sestiere*, as well as the house number, which confusingly relates to the neighbourhood rather than the street. Looking out for a local landmark and knowing the nearest vaporetto stop also helps.

Venetian dialect
Talk of the town

La Serenissima, the most serene republic of Venice, was autonomous for 1,000 years before falling to Napoleonic forces in the late 18th century. It only became part of Italy in 1866, five years after the rest of the country had been brought together.

The Venetian dialect is a powerful reminder of the city's independence and distinct identity. About two thirds of its 50,000 inhabitants continue to speak it today.

The language is a part of the land, as well as something that's used to describe it: today the island is complete with countless *calli* (streets), about 180 *rii* (small canals) and more than 400 bridges.

Venice Hotels

Hotels
—— Luxury lodgings

Venice is a city teeming with luxury hotels, many of which are grand, gilded and historic. Meanwhile, new spots are setting up shop all the time in order to accommodate the millions of tourists who descend each year. Yet not all are created equal and you don't always get what you pay for: some of the pricey spots can stray towards the ostentatious or even gaudy end of the spectrum. Luckily, tasteful glamour and a clutch of sleek, independent boutique options can still be found.

More importantly there are hotels that still have a firm focus on hospitality and will go out of their way to make you feel at home in a city of visitors. From distinguished palazzos with verdant grounds to serene canal-side B&Bs and modern apartments, there are a number of winsome options to hand. Read on to discover the best places to rest your head.

①
Cima Rosa, Santa Croce
Laidback lodgings

When it comes to hotels in Venice, the grand and showy are easy to find; less common are cosy, homely spots such as Cima Rosa. Opened in 2012 by US interior designer Brittany Hymore with the help of her Venetian architect husband Daniele Vallot (*both pictured*), this boutique bed and breakfast sits between a pretty courtyard and the Canal Grande.

Exposed beams and calm hues feature throughout the B&B, in which numerous pieces of furniture have been carefully restored by Hymore herself. With just five rooms – two of which are suites – spread over two floors, Cima Rosa can provide a tranquil respite. And while – obviously – your breakfast is taken care of, Hymore will also happily direct guests to her favourite restaurants if you're stuck for dinner ideas.
*1960 Calle del Forno, 30135
+39 041 863 302
cimarosavenezia.com*

MONOCLE COMMENT: An out-of-the-way location means Cima Rosa is near some lesser-known spots worth a look. For example, check out the Scuola Grande di San Rocco, brimming with 16th-century paintings by Tintoretto.

Venice — Hotels

Drink it all in — The terrace here is a cocktail hotspot

2
Bauer Venezia, San Marco
Rare find

Amid all of Venice's grand palazzos, the fascist-era modern façade of the Bauer's Campo San Moisè entrance sets it apart from the moment you lay eyes on it. The 18th-century building first opened its doors as a hotel in the 1880s but when the property changed ownership in the 1930s a new modern wing was built (the side facing the canal still boasts a Byzantine-gothic exterior).

Inside, the sleek marble lobby and sumptuous staircase lead to classic Venetian rooms upstairs, complete with wall tapestries and Murano glass chandeliers. There are canal-side lounges in which to enjoy a drink and guests also have access to Settimo Cielo (Seventh Heaven): it's the highest terrace in Venice, where guests can eat breakfast while enjoying panoramic views of the city.
1459 Campiello San Moise, 30124
+39 041 520 7022
bauervenezia.com

MONOCLE COMMENT: Room styles vary between traditional Venetian and those with more contemporary touches, such as art deco furniture. Take your pick.

③
Aman Venice, San Polo
Home comforts

Many of the city's majestic hotels were once home to aristocrats and royalty and the Aman Venice is no exception; in fact, the Arrivabene family still lives on the top floor of the palazzo. And the hotel, which opened in 2013 and is managed by the Aman hotel group, aims to feel like a home to visitors as well. There is no reception desk or concierge to be seen when you enter and amid the array of classical frescoes you'll find contemporary furniture.

There are only 24 rooms within this sprawling property; the rest of the hotel is made up of common areas, including two gardens and a library. There is no formal restaurant: guests can order food, drinks and snacks anywhere they like, including – but not limited to – the yellow dining room.

Palazzo Papadopoli, 1364 Calle Tiepolo Baiamonte, 30125
+39 041 270 7333
aman.com/resorts/aman-venice

MONOCLE COMMENT: Many of the hotel's classical features are actually protected historical artefacts: the Alcova Tiepolo Suite boasts an original, cherubic fresco by Giovanni Battista Tiepolo, for example.

Best of both — This classical hotel has a modern twist

Venice
Hotels

Venice
Hotels

④
Hotel Danieli, San Marco
Prime palazzo

Perhaps the most storied hotel in a city brimming with them, this is a stately 210-room affair made up of three palazzos, the oldest of which dates back to the 14th century. The entrance from the Riva degli Schiavoni, just steps away from the Ponte dei Sospiri (Bridge of Sighs), leads neatly into an expansive gilded bar and lounge. It plays host to a grand piano and Murano glass chandeliers; it has also provided the setting for scenes in two James Bond films.

The first floor – known as the *piano nobile* in Italian palazzos, as the high-ceilinged spaces were where the principal family rooms were found – is where Danieli's largest suites are located. These include the Doge Dandolo Royal, which is dedicated to the 41st doge of Venice and features an original 18th-century fresco by Jacopo Guarana.
4196 Calle de le Rasse, 30122
+39 041 522 6480
danielihotelvenice.com

MONOCLE COMMENT: The Terrazza Danieli restaurant and a newer bistro are on the top floor, both with expansive terraces that have breathtaking views of the Bacino di San Marco.

Venice
Hotels

⑤
Casa Flora, San Marco
Perennial pad

Gioele Romanelli, the owner of a handful of Venetian hotels, opened this light-filled three-bedroom apartment in 2017 with the aim of providing something unique amid the city's opulent offerings. Under the watchful eye of architect Matteo Ghidoni from Salottobuono and Laura Sari, interior designer at Reveria, the space was created using typical Venetian materials in a contemporary way.

All the furniture in the sleek apartment has been custom-made by regional firms: the sofas and beds are by Berto, fabrics are from Rubelli and the dining table was made by Xilia, a nearby woodworking company.

As the name would suggest, Casa Flora is filled with greenery, giving the space a lived-in feel. Each of the three large bedrooms comes with its own bath and steam room, all featuring the mosaic-like palladiana terrazzo tiles that are a mainstay of many Venetian homes. The expansive kitchen and dining room are perfect for hosting large dinner parties; Venetian chefs can be hired to cater. This is the place to stay if you're looking to break away from the city's love of brocade and gilding.
2283A San Marco, 30124
+39 041 520 5844
casafloravenezia.com

MONOCLE COMMENT: Romanelli and his team are happy to assist with unique Venetian ventures, such as arranging visits with regional tailors and shoemakers.

Home comforts
Everything in Casa Flora is made in Italy

Respect your elders

Across the street from Casa Flora is its big sister: Hotel Flora. It's more traditional than the newer site – though it's been updated over the past few decades – and its gorgeous garden courtyard remains intact. The perfect place to start your day with a cappuccino.

Venice Hotels

6
JW Marriott Venice Resort & Spa, Sacca Sessola
Take a step back

While cruising up to a hotel entrance via boat is an option in many spots across Venice, it's mandatory at the JW Marriott: the sprawling resort occupies the island of Sacca Sessola, a 10-minute journey across the lagoon from Piazza San Marco. But don't let the distance put you off: opened in 2015 and built by architect Matteo Thun, this sprawling 266-room hotel boasts four restaurants, three swimming pools, tennis courts, a gourmet food shop and the superb Goco Spa (*see page 124*).

There is plenty to keep you occupied without ever having to leave the grounds but getting back into the hubbub of Venice is no trouble: the resort lays on regular water taxi services to Piazza San Marco.
Isola delle Rose, 30133
+39 041 852 1300
jwvenice.com

MONOCLE COMMENT: Check out the rooftop pool and bar for stunning views of not only the island itself but also the ethereal Venetian skyline from a distance.

Venice
Hotels

⑦
Al Ponte Antico, Cannaregio
Opulent option

Venture down a cobblestone path past the Fondaco dei Tedeschi shopping centre and you'll find the lush Al Ponte Antico, a small and welcoming palazzo. The property has just nine rooms, augmented by a cosy (well-stocked) bar and lounge that has leather banquettes and a carefully restored ceiling. Prepare to get acquainted with other guests, as well as the owners: brothers Matteo and Bruno Peruch.

Al Ponte Antico's high-ceilinged rooms are done up with velvet tapestries. Without a doubt the hotel's best spot is its tiny yet elegant Canal Grande-side terrace, which offers picture-postcard views.
*5768 Calle dell'Aseo Cannaregio, 30131
+39 041 241 1944
alponteantico.com*

MONOCLE COMMENT: The Al Ponte Antico doesn't have a restaurant (although it does serve breakfast) but there are plenty of spots nearby.

You could top and tail?

Venice Hotels

(8) Hotel Metropole, San Marco
Unusually appealing

Hotel Metropole's location in the heart of the Riva degli Schiavoni promenade shouldn't fool you into thinking that this is any ordinary Venetian hotel. The 16th-century palazzo, once home to a girls' orphanage and music school, is now an eclectic spot with warm and quirky touches; 67 rooms are filled with plush furnishings and antique pieces.

Proprietor Gloria Beggiato, whose family has owned the property for generations, has added her own personal collections – from the charming (antique business-card cases) to the odd (corkscrews) – into the mix, all displayed in glass cabinets in the corridors. Don't let the unusual touches put you off, not least because the secluded Citrus Garden is a lovely spot to unwind with an aperitivo after a day of traversing Venice's narrow streets.
4149 Riva degli Schiavoni, 30122
+39 041 520 5044
hotelmetropole.com

MONOCLE COMMENT: The hotel's cocktail bar displays work made by a revolving roster of Venetian artists and is open to passers-by.

Good spirits — Be sure to visit the cocktail bar

Always famous

When it comes to hotels, Venice has its fair share of household names. Historical hotspots such as The Gritti Palace in San Marco, Belmond Hotel Cipriani on Giudecca and Ca' Sagredo Hotel in Cannaregio may not be new on the scene but they continue to live up to their reputations.

Hotels outside the city

01 Quattro Fontane, Lido: A quaint four-star hotel filled with antique furniture; outside there's a spacious garden and tennis courts.
quattrofontane.com

02 Grande Albergo Ausonia & Hungaria, Lido: Built in the early 20th century, with nods to art nouveau. Check out the spa and wellness centre.
hungaria.it

03 Venissa, Mazzorbo: Venissa is renowned for its food offering with both an osteria and Michelin-starred restaurant on-site (*see page 127*). There are six rooms upstairs, as well as a number of rooms scattered across restored houses on neighbouring Burano.
venissa.it

Venice — Hotels

⑨ Ca Maria Adele, Dorsoduro
Love is in the air

Nestled alongside the imposing Santa Maria della Salute, one of Venice's largest churches, Ca Maria Adele looks unassuming from the outside – yet inside the low-lit and intimate 14-room hotel makes for a charming bolthole. Hotelier brothers Alessio and Nicola Campa opened the property in 2004 and have mixed sumptuous interiors, classic Venetian sensibilities and touches of modern design to make this a romantic spot.

Meanwhile, the Collezione Peggy Guggenheim is just around the corner and there's also a roof terrace, where guests can take in the views of Venice with a cheeky glass of prosecco.
111 Rio Terrà Catecumeni, 30123
+39 041 520 3078
camariaadele.it

MONOCLE COMMENT: This is an adults-only affair. For those with small children, Ca Maria Adele offers an apartment suite.

⑩ Palazzo Venart, Santa Croce
Personal touch

This 15th-century palazzo, only recently repurposed as a hotel, sets itself apart with its service. General manager Angelo Rizzi (*pictured*), a hospitality veteran with years spent at the Hotel Principe di Savoia in Milan, prides himself on knowing how much – or how little – attention to lavish on visitors. "We're small so we know all the guests," he says. "People feel they can ask for anything."

The switched-on staff are on hand to help with whatever you might need, from a five-course dinner to help planning a romantic gesture. The Venart's location on the Canal Grande and its pretty garden don't hurt either.
1948A Calle Tron, 30135
+39 041 523 3784
palazzovenart.com

MONOCLE COMMENT: Dine indoors or alfresco at the restaurant, run by Michelin-starred Enrico Bartolini.

Venice
Food and drink

Food and drink
— Buon appetito

Restaurants
Where to eat

Although it's true that tourist traps taint Venice's reputation, you won't find any on these pages. Instead we've distilled the city's larger-than-life eating-and-drinking culture into a series for all appetites – from informal lunches to intimate dinners and late-night drinks.

Reliable traditional restaurants stand next to a new generation of restaurateurs who are blending familiar flavours with modern accents. Don't expect lots of pizza and lasagne: Venice is more about seafood. And book ahead, for the size of dining rooms and high demand allow for little improvisation.

Venice's iconic *bàcari* (backstreet bars) are keystones of food culture and dispensers of *cichèti* (small snacks), spritz and wine. We've selected a mix of century-old institutions and hip bars that colour outside the lines.

To round it all off we've included a string of top-tier cafés, markets, pastry shops and gelaterias to help you stay fuelled. We hope you're hungry.

①
CoVino, Castello
Small is beautiful

CoVino was founded by Andrea Lorenzon (*pictured, above*) and Cesare Benelli, owner and chef of Al Covo (*see opposite*). It's beloved by locals and visitors alike for its first-rate food, noteworthy wines and warm, *bàcaro*-style atmosphere.

Six tables make up the dining area, which is buzzy yet relaxed as chef Dimitri Gris (*pictured, left*) concocts an elaborate three-course menu. The selection of wines compiled by Lorenzon is superb and, a rarity in Venice, fish and meat get an equal look in.
3829A Calle del Pestrin, 30122
+39 041 241 2705
covinovenezia.com

Venice
Food and drink

❷ Osteria Bancogiro, San Polo
Grande standing

Longstanding *bàcaro*-cum-restaurant Osteria Bancogiro benefits from a prime location at the foot of the Ponte di Rialto; its back door opens onto a terrace graced by a glimpse of the Canal Grande.

Downstairs the wine bar dispenses clever *cichèti*, ranging from the classic to the curious, to be paired with various wines. Upstairs the unfussy brick-vaulted restaurant dishes out Venetian food with a twist: the pasta with cocoa-scented ragu and the veal cheek with polenta and artichokes are just a couple of highlights.
122 Campo San Giacometto, 30125
+ 39 041 523 2061
osteriabancogiro.it

❸ Al Covo, Castello
Make it modern

Run by Venetian chef Cesare Benelli and his American wife Diane (*both pictured*), Al Covo has set the standard for sophisticated Venetian cuisine since 1987, turning out classics with a modern touch. The restaurant is devoted to sourcing the best ingredients from the region and never loses sight of its sustainability ethos. Small-scale producers from the lagoon islands are favoured and even the provenance of the extra-virgin olive oil used is considered with care.

The ever-evolving menu is based around fresh ingredients that are masterfully prepared and creatively plated. Most dishes are based on market availability and standouts include the raw seafood platter and the *baccalà* (salted cod) with Biancoperla polenta. Save room for dessert: Diane's chocolate cake is unmissable.
3968 Calle de la Pescaria, 30122
— 39 041 522 3812
ristorantealcovo.com

I see you still have some spare tentacles, more dishes please...

② F Venice
Food and drink

④ Osteria Da Fiore, San Polo
Subtle elegance

Osteria Da Fiore, led by Mara and Maurizio Martin, is a chic Michelin-starred restaurant that began as a humble tavern before evolving into a fine-dining institution. Immaculate tablecloths and colourful Murano glassware brighten the traditional dining room, while the menu is centred on fresh seafood.

The six-course tasting menu at dinner offers the ideal sensorial journey. Look out for delicacies such as fried oysters with zabaione sauce, as well as squid-ink risotto and – in season – soft-shell crab.
2202A San Polo, 30125
+39 041 721 308
dafiore.net

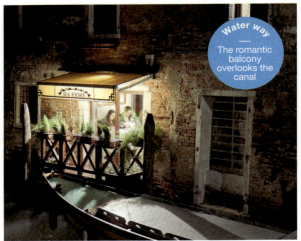

Water way — The romantic balcony overlooks the canal

⑤ Osteria alle Testiere, Castello
In-demand dining

It's notoriously tough to get a table at Alle Testiere, which is as famous for its 22-seat dining room as it is for fine fish. The demand is such that it has two sittings for dinner; booking for the later one at 21.00 will allow for a more leisurely meal in this soberly elegant osteria.

Swinging by the dark tables, sommelier Luca di Vita (*pictured*) guides guests around a well-formed list of Italian labels. In the kitchen chef Bruno Gavagnin's imaginative seafood dishes are equally inspired by the catch of the day and Venice's spice-trading tradition.
5801 Calle del Mondo Novo, 30122
+39 041 522 7220
osterialletestiere.it

Venice
Food and drink

> ### Pizza night
> For a break from *cichèti* and prosecco, Birraria La Corte, situated in a former brewery and with outdoor seating in Campo San Polo, serves a tempting assortment of pizza, beer and snacks in an informal, family-friendly setting.
> *birrarialacorte.it*

⑦ Ristorante Quadri, San Marco
Square meal

The Alajmo brothers, who earned their spot in the culinary firmament with their celebrated Le Calandre in Padua, have masterminded the revival of this historical establishment in Piazza San Marco. The restaurant – on the first floor, above the Grancaffè, also owned by the Alajmos – creates a lavish mood with a view of the piazza.

Chefs Silvio Giavedoni and Sergio Preziosa, along with Max Alajmo, have developed two tasting and à la carte menus that offer contemporary versions of traditional dishes. Worth the price.
121 Piazza San Marco, 30124
+39 041 522 2105
alajmo.it

⑥ Osteria Enoteca Ai Artisti, Dorsoduro
One for lovers

Despite its amorous reputation, Venice is in short supply of romantic restaurants. Ai Artisti is an exception, offering impeccable food in an intimate setting.

The place is minuscule: eight tables inside with three more outside in summer. The menu, devised by co-owners Francesca Ciancio and Vincenzo Buonfiglio and Japanese chef Masahiro Homma, has seasonal dishes that taste at once surprising and reassuringly recognisable.
1169A Fondamenta della Toletta, 30123
+39 041 523 8944
enotecaaartisti.com

Venice
Food and drink

9
Local, Castello
All in the name

Opened in 2015 by Luca and Benedetta Fullin (*both pictured*), whose family has run the nearby Hotel Wildner since the 1960s, Local's focus is on – naturally – local, seasonal ingredients. These are sourced from satellite islands and cooked by Matteo Tagliapietra.

"My cuisine combines elements of Venice's illustrious culinary heritage with modern influences I acquired working at Noma and Nobu," says Tagliapietra. You'll find classic pennoni pasta with wild boar alongside chargrilled eel with mango miso and chicory.
3303 Salizzada dei Greci, 30122
+39 041 241 1128
ristorantelocal.com

8
Estro, Dorsoduro
For wine worshippers

Estro means "flair" or "whim", two words that aptly describe the atmosphere of this gastronomic gem in the heart of artsy Dorsoduro. Run by exuberant siblings Alberto and Dario Spezzamonte, it's a casual wine-and-*cichèti* bar that's perfect for a quick stop-off or a meal with a group of friends.

By day it offers carefully chosen natural wines – bubbles come in hand-blown chalices by Murano glass master Elia Toffolo – while at night it doubles as a restaurant, serving popular contemporary dishes and meat, cheese and seafood platters. While chef Alberto's creations are pleasing to both the eye and the palate, the highlight remains the stellar list of 500 vintages, which the knowledgeable and friendly staff will help you navigate.
3778 Calle Crosera, 30100
+39 041 476 4914
estrovenezia.com

Venice
Food and drink

Bàcari
Tipples and nibbles

Antiche Carampane, San Polo
Hidden treasure

This tiny trattoria serves some of the finest fish in Venice. It's hard to find – the only way you'll stumble upon it is if you're lost in the twists and turns of San Polo – but the food will compensate for your quest.
 A sign at the entrance states that this is no place for tourist fare: "No pizza, no lasagne, no menù turistico." The ever-changing menu, which nods to both tradition and innovation, is religiously spelt out at the table. Don't miss the paccheri pasta with home-smoked swordfish.
1911 Rio Terà de le Carampane, 30125
+39 041 524 0165
antichecarampane.com

Must-try
Tagliatelle di castagne con ragù d'anatra from Vini da Gigio, Cannaregio
Venice is known for its seafood but its poultry is also remarkable. At Vini da Gigio try duck as a velvety ragu with chestnut tagliatelle or roasted, as is customary on Burano.
vinidagigio.com

Cà' d'Oro Alla Vedova, Cannaregio
Rush for rissoles

One of Venice's oldest osterias, notorious for its bygone charm and brusque service, offers a concise menu of *cichèti* and traditional dishes. There are two ways to experience this *bàcaro*: either standing at the counter grazing on the nibbles or sitting at the tables and ordering the pasta.
 Regulars are more inclined to linger by the bar nursing their *ombra* (glass of wine) while waiting for the legendary *polpette* (meat rissoles) to appear from the kitchen. Snap up a few before they disappear and pair them with the inexpensive house red.
3912 Calle Cà d'Oro, 30121
+39 041 528 5324

031

Venice
Food and drink

Moor time
—
Al Timon has a boat on the adjacent canal

② Al Timon, Cannaregio
Sail in

A favourite hangout for students and younger residents, Al Timon becomes an unrivalled aperitivo hotspot when the weather obliges. At peak hours the adjoining pavement can get swamped but for the clever handful who arrive early there's a boat moored along the canal that doubles as an impromptu lounging area.

Al Timon claims to have "the best meat in Venice" but it also happens to have the most mesmerising crostini counter, which is constantly replenished with fresh combinations: prosciutto and figs, gorgonzola and radicchio, courgettes and pecorino, and more. If you're still hungry, full-scale plates are available to those who prefer to sit down. A special nod goes to the wine list, savvily sprinkled with organic options.
2754 Fondamenta dei Ormesini, 30121
+39 041 524 6166
timonvenezia.com

③ Cantine del Vino già Schiavi, Dorsoduro
Artsy, tasty chaos

It can feel like pandemonium outside this celebrated 19th-century *bàcaro*, where artsy academics, bohemian characters, students and gondoliers gather for their daily fare. But it's always of the merry kind.

The bottle-lined room boasts an inviting spread of *cichèti*, all of which are prepared by Alessandra De Respinis (*pictured*) using ingredients such as mortadella and *baccalà mantecato* (salt-cod mousse). Things get hectic at lunchtime but you can kick back outside.
992 Fondamenta Nani, 30123
+39 041 523 0034
cantinaschiavi.com

Venice
Food and drink

④
Bacareto Da Lele, Santa Croce
Bargain buns

Located minutes from the bus terminal, this corner bar is where students on a budget congregate at all hours (it's open from 06.00) for stand-up drinks and scrumptious sandwiches, both dispensed at bargain prices. Da Lele's *paninetti* are laden with just about whatever strikes your fancy, from sundried tomatoes and artichokes to porchetta and burrata.

Prices are reasonable and despite the lack of comforts – the balustrade along the canal is the only place to sit down – the sociable service and campus-like atmosphere will help when it comes to unwinding.
183 Campo dei Tolentini, 30121

⑤
Cantina Do Mori, San Polo
Old school

This traditional *bàcaro* has been dispensing dishes of food and goblets of wine to Venetians since 1462. What makes it special is its ambience: vintage copper pots hang from the ceiling and the space is kitted out with well-worn dark-wood furniture, making it particularly picturesque.

Brightening things up is a symphony of sandwiches and *cichèti*, including the likes of artichoke hearts and eggs topped with anchovies. Doors open in the early morning but unless you like breakfasting on wine (as diehard Venetians do), pop in from 10.00.
429 Calle Do Mori, 30125
+ 39 041 522 5401

Food markets

01 **Mercato di Rialto, San Polo:** Open Tuesday to Saturday from 07.00 to noon, Venice's historical market is a food-shopping destination for chefs, residents and tourists.

02 **Mercato del Carcere Femminile, Giudecca:** A weekly market (Thursday, 09.00 to 12.00) of organic fruit and vegetables grown in the Giudecca women's detention centre. Much-loved for its ethos and unmatched freshness.

03 **Floating greengrocers, citywide:** Across the city you'll find floating barges selling fruit and vegetables, just as they did during the city's golden age. Those near Ponte dei Pugni and Via Garibaldi are popular.

Venice
F Food and drink

6
Ostaria Al Ponte, Cannaregio
Full board

Not to be confused with another tavern of the same name, this osteria is immediately identifiable by its bright-red wooden frontage and peculiar position halfway up a bridge leading to Basilica dei Santi Giovanni e Paolo. Wander in and head for the tables: unlike other *bàcari* in town, the layout of Al Ponte will actually allow for a sit-down snacking session, which is particularly pleasant after a long day's strolling. The presence of so many residents is also an indication of its authenticity.

Recently renovated, Al Ponte serves a popular choice of *cichèti*, as well as a wide selection of cured meat and cheese. Try the *carne salada* (cured salted beef) and the *sopressa* (garlic salami), or better still order a couple of the mixed sharing boards for a taste of what's best.
6378 Calle Larga Giacinto Gallina, 30121
+39 041 520 2747

7
La Cantina, Cannaregio
Creative crostini

The bite-sized *cichèti* found in other *bàcaro* are often prepared in advance and set out under glass for people to choose from. At La Cantina, however, *cichèti* are made to order by one-man wonder Francesco Zorzetto, who creates them on a whim using combinations and ingredients you won't find elsewhere.

There's no menu so it's best to just state your general preference (aside from crostini, raw fish is also a speciality) and then put yourself in Zorzetto's hands while you find some reprieve from Strada Nova's hordes in a glass of local wine.
3689 Campo San Felice, 30121
+39 041 522 8258

8
I Rusteghi, San Marco
Quality pioneers

"The best part of my job is the smile on people's faces as they exit the front door," says Giovanni D'Este, the passionate *oste* (host) behind I Rusteghi. Open since 1990, this gourmet osteria frequented by chefs and wine mavens is distinguished by the rarity of its ingredients, all carefully selected by D'Este.

Here cheese comes from pastured cows and the charcuterie is artisan. Both are best savoured in the most unadulterated way: atop a slice of rustic bread. Pure pleasure for the palate.
5513 Corte del Tentor, 30100
+39 338 760 6034
airusteghi.com

⑨ All'Arco, San Polo
Cichèti institution

No Venetian city break should come to an end without a visit to this flag-bearer of Venetian *cichèti* culture. Concealed under an arch (hence the name) just minutes from the fish market, All'Arco is a standing-only *bàcaro* with friendly lunchtime vibes and archetypal snacks such as *folpetti* (baby octopus), *sarde in saor* (sweet-and-sour sardines) and crostini aplenty.

Getting busy behind the bar is owner Francesco Pinto, who can be seen slicing cured meats and pressing panini, or pouring glass after glass of the house verduzzo or prosecco.
436 Calle Arco, 30125
+39 041 520 5666

Must-try
Scartosso de pesse from Acqua e Mais, San Polo
Scartosso de pesse, a paper cone filled with a fragrant medley of freshly fried fish and vegetables, has forever been synonymous with street food in Venice. Some call it the Italian equivalent of fish and chips. Acqua e Mais keeps the tradition alive by turning out piping-hot snacks to hungry passers-by. The cones are outrageously addictive so a return visit for seconds is highly likely.
acquaemais.com

Venice
Food and drink

Lunch
Midday repast

Grand view — The ideal spot to watch the gondolas go by

② Corte Sconta, Castello
Alfresco eats

Come here when the season allows you to eat outdoors because a leisurely lunch in the vine-roofed *corte sconta* (hidden courtyard) is undoubtedly the best way to enjoy the food and atmosphere of this unfussy restaurant.

Don't expect surprises though: the cuisine here is traditional and heavy on seafood such as mixed-fish platters and squid-ink pasta. Every dish is skilfully prepared without much adornment but with the freshest ingredients from the Mercato di Rialto.
3886 Calle del Pestrin Castello, 30122
+39 041 522 7024
cortescontavenezia.it

① Vinaria, San Polo
Modern vibes

Inside a refurbished Venetian palazzo, a stone's throw from the busy pavements of the Ponte di Rialto, Vinaria is a conceptual restaurant that offers refined modernist cuisine alongside gourmet pizzas, burgers and *cichèti*.

The connection between them is the finest ingredients: everything from Cantabrian anchovies to locally grown greens is handled creatively by chef Serghei Hachi. Though guests come for the food, the beautiful interiors and tall windows opening onto the Canal Grande are part of the attraction.
1097 Riva del Vin, 30125
+39 041 241 0465
vinariaristorante.it

Palazzo lunching

As well as first-class exhibits, Palazzo Franchetti also has a welcoming cafeteria, which at lunchtime offers a rich buffet accessible to all for a fixed price. The neo-gothic arches, large Murano chandeliers and an inner garden complete the experience.
palazzofranchetti.it

Venice
Food and drink

 Osteria Anice Stellato, Cannaregio
Spice up your life

Located alongside a canal in the more laidback area of Cannaregio, this attractive family-run osteria has gained a solid reputation for its good food, casual ambience, fair prices and cordial (yet never overly ceremonious) service.

The menu is a clever combination of quintessentially Venetian seafood and some meat dishes, many of which are made with intriguing ingredients. The name (*anice stellato* is a star anise) hints at the city's spice-dealing heritage and the dishes reflect this: marinated prawns in *saor* (sweet-and-sour sauce) are scented with ginger and pink pepper, while pasta sauces contain touches of cinnamon and nutmeg.

At the back, the peaceful alfresco terrace offers a rare chance to relax in a quieter corner away from the tourist bustle.
3272 Fondamenta de la Sensa, 30121
+39 041 720 744
osterianicestellato.com

Gourd news
—
'La zucca' is Italian for pumpkin

③
La Zucca, San Polo
Vegetarian choices

Don't let the Alpine chalet-style interior fool you: this cosy osteria is as Venetian as it gets. The clue is as much in the green shutters and canal setting – particularly picturesque during the day – as it is in the food.

Although not a meat-free restaurant, La Zucca is famous for its vegetarian leanings (a rarity in Venice) and affords some respite from fish with its vast array of vegetable-based options. These range from seasonal appetisers to heart-warming pasta and specialities such as asparagus flan with parmesan fondue. Carnivores, don't despair: meat dishes vary from heirloom to fusion and often include lesser-known cuts. In season, everyone should try the signature *flan di zucca*: a light pumpkin delight topped with grated cheese and seeds.
1762 Calle dello Spezier, 30135
+39 041 524 1570
lazucca.it

Must-try dishes
Tramezzini from Bar alla Toletta, Dorsoduro
Tramezzini are triangular sandwiches made with soft, crustless bread coated with mayonnaise and stuffed with all manner of fillings; this snack bar offers an imaginative selection.
1191 Dorsoduro, 30123

Venice
F Food and drink

Food and drink connoisseurs

01 Casa del Parmigiano, San Polo: The Aliani family has been selling cheese and charcuterie to the food connoisseurs of Venice since 1936. This is where the best parmigiano in town can be found, along with other regional cheeses. Choose between everything from buffalo mozzarella to taleggio, or head to the bountiful cured-meat counter.
aliani-casadelparmigiano.it

02 La Bottega del Gusto, Dorsoduro: This unflashy family-run delicatessen stocks all sorts of temptations, from fresh pasta to *baicoli* (crisp Venetian biscuits), roasted meat and pickled peppers. Ideal for a picnic or some edible souvenirs to take back home.

03 Millevini, San Marco: Lorenzo Menegus founded Millevini in 2002 after working in wine bars and wineries across the Veneto region. His experience is reflected in the remarkable selection of his *enoteca*, which has an array of Italian wines and spirits, including organic, biodynamic and ethically produced labels to suit all pockets.

Grab a goodie

Rosa Salva is a big name on the catering scene and still the place to head if you're organising a party. It's also known for its series of pastry shops across the city. Head to one of six locations for excellent sweets and moreish *tramezzini*.
rosasalva.it

Sweet treats
Speciality pick-me-ups

①
Pasticceria Dal Mas, Cannaregio
Breakfast bustle

Minutes away from the railway station and welcoming a constant stream of commuters, residents and day-trippers, Pasticceria Dal Mas is strong on typical Venetian biscuits and shortcakes, from *zaleti* (polenta raisin biscuits) to *fregolotta* (a crumbly tart with almonds). It also stands out for its vast breakfast spread, featuring dozens of pastries and brioches.

Goods are made in-house using fresh ingredients, unlike the baked-from-frozen stuff elsewhere. Take away a tray of the assorted pastries to turn teatime into a feast.
149A Rio Terà Lista di Spagna, 30121
+ 39 041 715 101
dalmaspasticceria.it

②
Pasticceria Tonolo, Dorsoduro
Worth the wait

Nestled in Dorsoduro's gastronomic hub, Tonolo is Venice's hotspot for pastries of all shapes and sizes. Don't be discouraged by the crowds that gather around this tiny shop as the queue moves fast; grab your order then move outside to savour your pastry in peace.

The crowds are even larger during Carnevale, when Tonolo plays to one of its strengths and sets out large trays full of fried *frittelle* (Venetian doughnuts) that are either plain, apple-laced or cream-filled. These are hugely sought after so act fast to secure your cut.
3764 Calle San Pantalon, 30100
+ 39 041 523 7209

③ VizioVirtù Cioccolateria, Castello
Chocolate alchemy

VizioVirtù opened in 2005 and has been the sleekest chocolate shop in town ever since. Self-taught chocolatier Mariangela Penzo is the brains behind the operation, which fuses Venice's love for spice with modern techniques.

Penzo's smartly displayed painterly creations are downright seductive, with hundreds of types of pralines, bars and chocolate-coated dried fruits (the figs are particularly good). Don't resist the lure of the truffles; as the old adage goes, the only way to rid yourself of temptation is to yield to it.
5988 Calle Forneri, 30122
+ 39 041 275 0149
viziovirtu.com

④ Pasticceria Rizzardini, San Polo
All-time favourite

This eye-catching *pasticceria* (pastry shop), now led by affable owner Paolo Garlato, has been turning out sweets since 1742 – hence the impressive period interiors. Rizzardini specialises in traditional Venetian pastries, cakes and biscuits and does so with showstopping results. So much so that the pillowy cream puffs and, in season, the sugar-coated Carnevale *frittelle* attract a faithful following.

Special mention goes to the *torta di ricotta* and the marzipan cake. This is definitely the place to head for a post-lunch sugar fix.
1415 Calle dei Meloni, 30125
+ 39 041 522 3835

Rising star

Since 1956, Franco "Nono" Colussi has produced *fugassa*: a light, sugar-crusted, brioche-like delight (the best in town, according to many), which is naturally leavened using a 65-year-old sourdough starter for authentic results. Head to his Dorsoduro bakery to try it.
dalnonocolussi.com

Gelaterias

01 Gelatoteca Suso, San Marco: Tucked away in a moody *sotopòrtego* (passageway), shouting distance from the Ponte di Rialto, this artisan gelateria churns both classic and innovative flavours using premium ingredients. We'd recommend the dark-chocolate sorbet and the salted pistachio.
suso.gelatoteca.it

02 Gelateria il Doge, Dorsoduro and San Polo: This award-winning gelateria in Campo Santa Margherita will have you spoiled for choice when it comes to selecting a flavour. Its *crema del Doge* – a rich custard base with candied citrus and chocolate – is a speciality.
gelateriaildoge.com

03 Gelateria Nico, Dorsoduro: Among the many reasons to love this old-fashioned parlour are its setting on the serene Zattere and the fact that you can enjoy your gelato on the terrace. Another plus is the signature *gianduiotto*: hazelnut-chocolate semifreddo under an avalanche of cream.
gelaterianico.com

Venice
Food and drink

Coffee
Espresso service

① **Caffè Girani, Castello**
Fine beans

Established by Giuseppe Girani in 1928, this small family-operated coffee roaster set in a carefully preserved 18th-century workshop is the only place that residents and coffee connoisseurs will consider for their supplies. Today a mother-and-daughter team processes and roasts single arabica and robusta bean varieties separately before starting the secret-recipe blending, so as to obtain a consistent product that has few rivals. The Casanova gourmet blend is a favourite but only available when a particular bean can be sourced.

Caffè Girani doesn't brew coffee on site but it does sell blends to the public and supplies many of Venice's top hotels and restaurants. You'll often receive a complimentary lesson on how to prepare *un buon caffè* at home when you buy beans in the shop.
3727 Calle del Dose, 30122
+ 39 041 721 500
caffegirani.it

② **Goppion Caffetteria, Cannaregio**
Casual coffee break

With headquarters near the town of Treviso, this fifth-generation roaster has established a reputation on the city's coffee scene thanks to its well-crafted blends. Two cafés (one in San Polo), situated on busy thoroughfares near the train station and the Mercato di Rialto, ensure a steady stream of customers.

The mood is friendly but fast-paced so don't expect a leisurely time perusing the colourful Bialetti percolators on sale. The Cannaregio branch has a few outdoor seats to kick off your shoes and take things a tad slower.
1185E Calle del Pistor, 30121
+ 39 041 714 232
goppioncaffe.it

Venice
Food and drink

Coffee lover
Caffè Florian was a favourite haunt of Casanova

③ Caffè Florian, San Marco
Timeless and classy

Iconic but expensive, Florian is the oldest café in Italy (in business since 1720) and takes you back to an era of smart waiters and frescoed ceilings. Venetians in the mood for a splurge stand at the bar, while other patrons tend to be visitors wanting an extravagant experience.

Avoid the urge to sit outside as the tunes played by the quintet come at a surcharge. Instead take a table in one of the rococo tearooms and try the *cioccolata con panna* (dark hot chocolate with whipped cream) or, in summer, a frothy *caffè shakerato* (iced coffee).
57 *Piazza San Marco, 30124*
+39 041 520 5641
caffeflorian.com

Caffè culture

As the gateway for coffee into Europe in the 17th century and host to the oldest café in Italy – the luxurious Caffè Florian (*see left*) – Venice takes its caffeine very seriously. Not only is it still home to a good number of established coffee roasters but many of them have now opened their operations to the public, either selling beans or brewing espressos.

Like the rest of the country, Venetians apply important rules to the business of coffee consumption. For instance, milky coffees larger than a macchiato are not to be ordered after midday unless you want to be labelled a clueless tourist. Likewise cappuccino with savoury food is a no-no. And if you just want a shot of espresso simply ask for *un caffè*. No specifications needed unless you want a *doppio* (double), which is acceptable but not customary as Venetians tend to get their daily caffeine intake in small, frequent increments.

Finally, if you really want to feel like a native, drink your coffee at the counter and forget table service: it's cheaper, quicker and better. Takeaway is rarely an option: a hot ceramic cup and two gulps on the spot is the way to go.

I always drink my coffee standing up, like a true Venetian

Venice
Food and drink

Drinks
Cin cin

④
Torrefazione Cannaregio,
Cannaregio
Blend in

This coffee roaster has been keeping Cannaregio caffeinated since it opened in 1930. There are no seats, just a long wooden counter and a back wall of vintage containers filled with a handpicked selection of speciality coffee blends to either experience on the spot or take away by the bagful. Its trademark Cafè Remèr blend, made with a combination of eight arabica varieties, merits a special mention.

Make your way to the front, take your pick and watch the person behind the bar prepare your cappuccino or chosen caffè with the ease and diligence of a real expert. It's a popular place so you won't be able to linger for long but you'll be tempted to come back again and again.
*1337 Rio Terà San Leonardo, 30121
+39 041 716 371
torrefazionecannaregio.it*

Standing room — Take your drink and mingle in the square

⑤
Al Mercà, San Polo
Bijou happy hour

Conveniently cocooned in a *campo* behind the Mercato di Rialto, Al Mercà springs to life at aperitivo time – from 11.00 to 14.00 and 18.00 to 20.00 – when thirsty folk gather in convivial spirits. The place is tiny but packs a lot into its limited square footage.

Spritz is always an option and there's a good choice of regional wines (try the prosecco col fondo) poured by friendly bartenders. Food-wise, the snack case filled with mini sandwiches and rissoles provides sustenance for the peckish but beware: they sell out quickly.
*213 Campo Bella Vienna, 30125
+39 346 834 0660*

Venice
Food and drink

② Skyline Rooftop Bar, Giudecca
High-rise cocktails

Perched at the top of the imposing Molino Stucky – a former flour mill, now home to a Hilton hotel – this futuristic, fluorescent rooftop bar on Giudecca is far from understated. But as its name suggests, what the Skyline Rooftop Bar lacks in subtlety it more than makes up for with its spectacular view of the city. Pull up a seat by the pool alongside the fashionable set and enjoy a cocktail looking out over the Canale della Giudecca to San Marco.

"Each of our cocktails possesses a trait that embodies the spirit of Venice," says bar manager Enrico Fuga (*pictured*). "We wanted the drinks menu to be a sensory journey through the city's enchanting *sestieri*." Prices are in line with the stature of the setting and include a complimentary boat service from the main island.
810 Via Giudecca, 30133
+39 041 272 3316
skylinebarvenice.com

③ Vino Vero, Cannaregio
A cut above

With its minimal interior, exceptional wines and interesting nibbles, Vino Vero is an exciting addition to Venice's drinking scene and sits easily next to its many good neighbours. The exposed brick wall in Matteo Bartoli's bar and shop is lined with a superior selection of small-scale Italian labels. The affordable by-the-glass wine list rotates a handful of bottles every day and the *cichèti* made here are a cut above the usual fare with more unconventional toppings. It gets packed at peak hours but never unpleasantly so.
2497 Fondamenta Misericordia, 30100
+39 041 275 0044

Nightlife hub

You'll be hard pressed to find many bars open past midnight in the city but Chet Bar, Ai Do Draghi and Bollicine, all around Campo Santa Margherita, are among the few to allow late drinking. Great for Venice's younger crowd and those looking for a nightcap.

Venice
Food and drink

④ Enoiteca Mascareta, Castello
Cheerful character

A bastion of Venice, not unlike the man at its helm – the exuberant, bow-tied Mauro Lorenzon (*pictured*) – this atmospheric *enoiteca* is now a respected restaurant. Even so, regulars, including chefs knocking off from their shifts at nearby establishments, continue to treat it like a wine bar and arrive late for one last glass (or three).

A chalkboard lists the wines available by the glass, most of them from northern Italy and all either natural, organic or biodynamic, according to the host's ethos. If you're unsure then ask Lorenzon for direction: he's a colourful character who takes the concept of hospitality very seriously and is genuinely keen to ensure his guests have the best drinking experience in the city.
5183 Calle Lunga Santa Maria Formosa, 30122
+39 041 523 0744
ostemaurolorenzon.it

Classic cocktails

Once Ernest Hemingway's favourite hangout, Harry's Bar is now a very busy and pricey affair. Nonetheless the buzz is worth the splurge. The bellini was invented here so by all means try one. The martinis are equally top-notch.
harrysbarvenezia.com

Venice
——— Food and drink

⑤
Paradiso Perduto, Cannaregio
Plain lively

Come rain, wind or high tide, there are always a few regulars who won't miss their appointment with the spritz and snacks of Paradiso Perduto. Situated in a more low-key part of Cannaregio, the bar's decor comprises mismatched chairs, dark wooden panels and tarnished tables but what it lacks in looks it more than makes up for in charisma.
   Spritz with Select is a must, as is a mixed plate from the plentiful fried-fish and *cichèti* counter. Pop by for aperitivo or later at night when, if you're lucky, you might catch one of its live jazz shows.
2540 Fondamenta della Misericordia, 30100
+39 041 720 581

⑥
El Sbarlefo San Pantalon, Dorsoduro
Smart sipping

This upgraded *bàcaro* has shaken up Venice's nightlife with well-stirred drinks and live concerts at the weekend. A minute's walk from Campo Santa Margherita, El Sbarlefo San Pantalon sports bright-yellow lights, pendant lamps and a sleek *cichèti* counter.
   Drinks range from spritzes to high-end cocktails, gins and whiskies, and there's also a good selection of wines. Pick a mix of *fritti* (such as tuna rissoles, fried cod and bass medallions), grab a seat and relax as day turns to night.
3757 Calle San Pantalon, 30123
+39 041 524 6650
elsbarlefo.it

The story of spritz

It's thought that the modern version of spritz – a mix of white sparkling wine, soda water and blush bitter liqueur – first appeared in Venice in the 1800s during the Austrian occupation. Although this popular aperitif is known internationally thanks to brands such as Aperol, which had the recipe acknowledged by the International Bartenders Association as a mix of Aperol, prosecco and seltzer, many variations exist in the city.
   It's not uncommon to see spritz stirred with Select – a local spirit with a red hue and a bitter accent – or served with a splash of Campari or Cynar. Venetians sip it any time of the day but as an aperitif, spritz is meant to precede a meal rather than go with it.

Retail
—— Merchants of Venice

Menswear
Man's world

With virtually every *calle* in the centre lined with little one-window shops, you'd be forgiven for thinking that Venice's retail scene is somewhat overcrowded. But don't be put off by the outlets that deal exclusively in knick-knacks of debatable quality: a generation of resilient shopkeepers and enterprising retailers has fought to maintain pockets of excellence in the least expected corners of this labyrinthine city.

Faithful to Venice's manufacturing tradition, tailors, shoemakers and printers are at work in their ateliers. Both emerging fashion designers and industry veterans gravitate to the city and use it as a constant source of inspiration for their experimental creations, while decades-old workshops painstakingly preserve age-old crafts.

Join us in meeting the hat-weaver who caters to the city's gondoliers and the interior designers who used to furnish Peggy Guggenheim's apartment. In Venice the best shop always awaits over the next bridge.

①
G Benevento, Cannaregio
Shop with history

Many of Italy's traditional *mercerie* (haberdashers stocking anything from ribbons to nighties) may have died out over the past century but this one survived. Founded in 1883 by Giacomo Benevento, it's now run by Giuseppe (*pictured*) and Francesco, his great-grandchildren.

Today it stocks a handsome selection of menswear, including coats by Hetregò, scarves by Altea and shirts by Xacus. Meanwhile, in the old *merceria* space, ceiling-high piles of multicoloured textiles routinely entice customers to order bespoke items.

3991/3945 Via Strada Nova, 30121
+ 39 041 522 0901
gbenevento.it

Material matters

Whatever your textile needs, G Benevento has you covered (with plenty of blankets and linen). Just hop across the road and directly opposite you'll find the homeware branch of this shop, which also stocks cushions, curtains and majestic velvet Venetian tapestries.

Venice — Retail

② Franco Puppato, San Marco
Trigonometric tailor

A narrow cul-de-sac may seem an unlikely spot for a tailor of international repute but it's here that Franco Puppato (*pictured*) opened his studio in 1964 – and here that he has remained.

Puppato deems himself the only living exponent of the trigonometric tailoring method (an unusual way of taking measurements, all from a single point on the chest). Suits are stitched with mathematical precision, each one taking about 65 hours to complete; the tailor has a suite next door should you want to wait.
4723 Calle dei Fabbri, 30124
+39 041 522 1814
francopuppato.it

③ Shirts & Ties, San Marco
Classic Italian

Despite its English name, Shirts & Ties deals in the very best classic Italian labels, from Aspesi to Herno, as well as a fair few Neapolitan staples by Sartoria Partenopea and Finamore.

Co-founder Attilio Vio opened this small venture a short walk from Piazza San Marco in 1995, together with business partner Fabio Vacher. The decor may not be standout but the savvy selection has garnered a loyal following – so much so that the founders have decided to open an outpost in London, where its moniker fits right in.
1279 Bocca di Piazza, 30124
+39 041 522 4948
shirtsandties.it

④ Al Duca d'Aosta, San Marco
More than just shirts

Emilio Ceccato founded a company that sold shirt fabric in 1902 and soon expanded his vision to produce the shirts as well. Ceccato later snagged the contract to clothe the city's gondoliers and then the business moved into menswear with multibrand chain Al Duca d'Aosta.

Today the latter has eight outposts across northern Italy, which sell top-quality brands such as Golden Goose and Marni. The most recent addition to the empire is its new flagship in San Marco, where you can find its eponymous in-house menswear line.
284 Calle Larga San Marco, 30124
+39 041 522 0733
alducadaosta.com

Family matters — Puppato and his wife, Emma, stitch the suits

Venice Retail

Womenswear
Fashion for her

Buosi Successori, San Marco
Modern traditional

First opened in the late 1800s, this shop has retained much of its old-school aura with its red carpets and dark wood-lined window cabinets. Employees Sergio Ferrarese (*pictured*) and Riccardo Bonometto took over the shop in 1974 and have been running it ever since, sticking to mainly Italian brands.

From Italo Ferretti's silk ties to shirts by Bottega Artigiana, the selection veers towards the classic. "Our style is traditional yet modern," says Ferrarese. Working with external tailors, the shop also offers bespoke shirts and suits.
5382/81 Campo San Bartolomeo, 30124
+39 041 520 8567

❶
Oh My Blue, San Polo
Style as art

You'd be forgiven for thinking that Oh My Blue on pretty Campo San Tomà is actually a contemporary-art gallery. Step inside, however, and you'll soon see that the plinths in this white-walled space are topped with jewellery and accessories rather than sculptures.

Designed by Venice-based Studio Tencalla, the tables and shelves can be rearranged to suit the ever-changing offering chosen by founder Elena Rizzi (*pictured*). As well as clothing and bags from Issey Miyake, you'll find hats by Italian brand Ilariusss and jewellery by Anna Norrgrann. All of the products in the shop are sourced by Rizzi on her worldly travels, which have taken her to the likes of Costa Rica and Japan. "Like Venice, this is a place where the world converges," she says.
2865 Campo San Tomà, 30125
+39 041 243 5741
ohmyblue.it

Venice — Retail

Luxury fashion brands manufacturing in the Veneto

The Veneto has been a hotspot for luxury brands since the boom in Venice's textiles industry in the 15th century and today the region continues to specialise in the production of high-end leather footwear for men and women.

01 Louis Vuitton: Given that the area is referred to as the cradle of luxury shoemaking, it's no surprise that in 1997 Louis Vuitton decided to buy a small family-run shoe factory in Fiesso d'Artico, just outside Venice, and take over production. The big-name brand incorporated the expertise of the craftsmen employed there, who do most of their work by hand.
louisvuitton.com

02 Prada: Just up the road in Dolo is the production plant for Prada. Tapping into the area's history of footwear manufacturing, the fashion label chose this as the site to turn out its women's shoes. Conveniently there's a luxury outlet shop nearby should you wish to pick up a pair or two.
prada.com

03 Christian Dior: While still located in the Veneto, Christian Dior's factory is about a 40-minute drive away in Selvazzano Dentro, Padua. The brand may be a heritage French name but its leather goods are well and truly made in Italy.
dior.com

② Kirikù, San Marco
Easy living

Founder Cristina Nogara had settled on a career in psychology but at the back of her mind there was always a desire to get into fashion. In 2003 she finally took the plunge and opened her own childrenswear shop; three years later the focus shifted to womenswear instead.

Kirikù, dotted with mid-century armchairs, is filled with clothes from up-and-coming Italian designers. It also stocks French shoes and Japanese socks but Nogara's whole selection has a lighthearted and bohemian feel.
1729 Frezzaria, 30124
+39 041 296 0619
kiriku.it

③ Noa di Nina, San Marco
Bohemian threads

A wooden-framed bed sits in the middle of womenswear shop Noa di Nina: it's an open invitation to while away some time in this warm but unstuffy space. Hanging on the walls are silk dresses and colourful cardigans, as well as formal wear by Lardini, while pretty shoes by the likes of Pomandère sit directly on the rough stone floor.

This lovely canal-side space is owner Daniela Soreca's second outpost; to find her original shop, Nina, you'll have to cross the Canal Grande and hop over to Campiello San Rocco.
Campo Manin, 30124
+39 041 822 1085

I'm all dressed, now where's my gondola?

Venice
Retail

④ Ottico Fabbricatore, San Marco
Eye for style

Francesco Lincetto is the "eyewear-maker" who gave Ottico Fabbricatore its name: in 1989 he turned this glasses shop into a revered womenswear boutique.

Lincetto's wife, fashion designer Marianna Leardini, originally provided the shop with a cashmere knitwear line, later adding silk clothes and soft leather bags; Lincetto's glasses and sunglasses also grace the shelves. Beyond an internal courtyard is a backroom furnished with velvet sofas that offers all manner of Italian women's brands, from underwear to outerwear.
4773 Calle del Lovo, 30124
+39 041 522 5263

⑤ Godi Fiorenza, San Marco
Sculptural styles

Readers of Dante's *Inferno* will recognise this shop's name as the beginning of Canto XXVI. It's also a reference to the surname of the shop's founders, Patrizia and Samanta Fiorenza, who started their own label in 1999.

While Patrizia (*pictured*) takes care of the sculptural clothing, Samanta focuses on accessories and jewellery. Often embellished with embroidery and sewn glass beads, the clothes are inspired by art, architecture and eastern Asia. All items are handmade in the back of the shop.
4261 Calle Minelli, 30124
+39 041 241 0866
fiorenzadesign.com

Mixed fashion
Something for everyone

① Barena Venezia, San Marco
Lagoon inspiration

This wood-clad shop is an intimate affair and while it only features a tight selection from Barena's line, it includes all of the signature pieces.

The typical *tabarro* – a heavy wool cape – is perhaps the brand's most Venetian design but all of its clothes draw inspiration from the lagoon, its sailors and fishermen. All pieces are made from high-end textiles and are eminently wearable.
4260B Calle Minelli, 30124
+39 041 523 8457
barenavenezia.com

Venice — Retail

② Altrove, San Polo
Experimental fashion

Miriam Nonino and Alessandra Milan founded Altrove in 2010 to create clothes that defy traditional boundaries; their boxy clothes encourage wearers to experiment and have fun. "You can wear them as you like, putting the front at the back or buttoning them in different ways," says Milan. "These are clothes to suit your mood."

The shop's monochrome decor accentuates exposed beams and brick walls lightly stained by lagoon water. And despite the name – *altrove* means "elsewhere" – each item is designed and made in Venice.
2659A Calle Moro, 30125
+ 39 041 476 4473
iosonoaltrove.com

③ Bottega Veneta, San Marco
Leather and more

Creative director Tomas Maier designed not just this shop's wares but also its interior. The space (once a pharmacy) opened in 2012 and features walnut tables, wool carpets and leather-covered handles.

A couple of hours' drive away on the mainland is the Bottega Veneta atelier, where artisans weave the strips of leather that make the brand's staple Intrecciato range, including the Olimpia bags and Knot clutches. At the San Marco shop, however, you'll find the label's full collection, from eyewear to fragrances.
1473 Salizada San Moisè, 30124
+ 39 041 522 8489
bottegaveneta.com

Hell for leather

Bottega Veneta's Scuola della Pelletteria (School of Leather-making) is located in the brand's atelier in Montebello Vicentino and serves as a workshop for employees to pass on their craft and expertise to the next generation of bagmakers.

Venice Retail

Homeware
Feather your nest

Chiarastella Cattana, San Marco
Carefully crafted linens

A long career in Milanese fashion convinced Chiarastella Cattana of her love for tactile textiles – but also of the need to forgo the breakneck speed of seasonal collections for a slower, more considered way of working. Her spacious shop in a quiet alley is a fitting home for her sophisticated finespun line. From tablecloths to towels, cushions to curtains, her understated cotton and linen designs are woven by artisans in the South Tyrol region or hand-embroidered by Venetians.

Cattana's geometric patterns are born from her observations of Venice's streets and each is available in 80 different hues. Nepal-inspired cashmere blankets and minimal drinking glasses have expanded the range: also on show are vintage Murano vases, as well as coats and jewellery by local designers she supports.
3216 Salizzada San Samuele, 30124
+ 39 041 522 4369
chiarastellacattana.com

Boselli, Dorsoduro
Furniture and art

This interior-design studio-cum-shop has hopped around the city. In 1960 it began life in Castello (Peggy Guggenheim was one of its clients) only to jump to Cannaregio and, later, Rialto. Since 2011 it has settled in a 19th-century warehouse on a quiet canal in Dorsoduro.

Beneath the high ceilings is a tight selection of sculptural furniture by Swiss, German and Finnish brands, as well as Italian heavy hitters such as Cassina, Alias and De Padova. The studio also doubles up as an exhibition space with an edgy show programme.
2241B Calle de la Madona, 30123
+ 39 041 522 2330
bosellivenezia.it

Venice
——— Retail

Murano glass

Don't be discouraged by the countless shopfronts selling mock-Muranese tat. On the small island off Venice proper, many companies are keeping the fires of traditional glass-making burning.

01 **Venini:** Perhaps the most established of the heritage Muranese brands thanks to its iconic designs by Carlo Scarpa, Tapio Wirkkala and Gio Ponti, Venini now collaborates with the likes of Tadao Ando and Ronan & Erwan Bouroullec on its imaginative glass products.
venini.com

02 **Salviati:** The rich archive of Salviati is ripe for rediscovery. Since young design collective Breaking the Mold was brought in to advise on creative matters, sensitive reinterpretations of catalogue classics have appeared on the shelves.
salviati.com

03 **Carlo Moretti:** Under the guidance of Antonio Ceschel and Manuel Gomiero, this big player has found its stride again. Its approach has tightened the catalogue to let the standout pieces shine, from cheerful glasses to elegant decorative vases.
carlomoretti.com

Madera, Dorsoduro
Modern designs

At Madera, owner Francesca Meratti has carved out a niche with her careful edit of contemporary design that relies on brands beyond Murano glass. Situated on Campo San Barnaba, her shop stocks pieces from Italian brands (including terracotta pots from Sambonet and the Gela carafe from Internoitaliano, designed by Massimo Barbierato), as well as more cutting-edge models such as KnIndustrie aluminium pans that double as bowls thanks to their detachable handles.
2729 Calle Lunga San Barnaba, 30123
+39 041 522 4181
maderavenezia.it

053

Venice
Retail

Specialist retail
Niche markets

Handmade paper — The shop uses antique Asian printing blocks

①
Legatoria Polliero, San Polo
Paper chase

This pint-sized bookbinding studio next to the Basilica di Santa Maria Gloriosa dei Frari (*see page 90*) has been run by the Polliero family since the 1930s. The founder's grandson, Anselmo Polliero, is now at the helm of the workshop and continues to carry out production true to the family's traditions.

All paper is still decorated by hand using three different techniques: silk-screen printing, wood-block printing and the signature Venetian technique of marbling. Materials, whether paper or leather, are sourced in Italy and made into tactile bound notebooks. "It takes us between three and four days to create a book," says Anselmo's mother Paola (*pictured*). Take a leaf from our book and stock up on all manner of stationery here; there's even some gold-leafed parchment should you ever need to pen an edict.
2995 Campo dei Frari, 30125
+ 39 041 528 5310

Venice — Retail

② Gabriele Gmeiner, San Polo
No mean feet

After stints with John Lobb in London and Hermès in Paris, Austrian shoemaker Gabriele Gmeiner (*pictured, above left*) moved to Venice to learn under one of the city's last surviving ateliers. In 2003 she opened a workshop for bespoke footwear: everything from men's Oxfords with Norwegian welt construction to ladies' boots.

Calfskin comes from France, cordovan from Mexico and vegetable-tanned soles from Germany's Rendenbach. It takes 12 months from the first fitting to the final product but it's worth the wait.

951 Campiello del Sol, 30125
+39 338 896 2189
gabrielegmeiner.com

③ ⓡ Venice — Retail

③
Gianni Basso Stampatore, Cannaregio
Press gang

Printer Gianni Basso learned his trade alongside the Armenian monks of San Lazzaro, who churned out books for more than two centuries.

Today, Basso and his son Stefano (*both pictured*) operate pre-industrial printing presses from the 1800s to make business cards, thank-you notes and books. They use manual typesetting and source Italy's highest-quality paper from Fabriano. Don't miss the exhibit that explores the history of etching, lithography and typography.
5306 Calle del Fumo, 30121
+39 041 523 4681

Traditional crafts

01 Annelie, Dorsoduro:
This shrine to lace is tucked away down Calle Lunga San Barnaba. From delicate sachets to embroidered nightgowns and linen tablecloths, it stocks lacework – including antique examples – with a focus on clothes and accessories for girls.
+39 041 520 3277

02 Ca' Macana, Dorsoduro:
While this mask shop was only born in 1984, its artisans use traditional techniques, hand-making the masks as they would have eight centuries ago. Created from clay, plaster and papier mâché, no two are the same.
camacana.com

03 Tessitura Luigi Bevilacqua, Santa Croce:
This family-run fabric business uses 18th-century looms. Its archives hold 3,500 designs, some of which have featured in the likes of the Oval Office and Stockholm city hall.
luigi-bevilacqua.com

Venice Retail

Custom craft — Each piece is made to suit a gondolier's height

I Muschieri, San Marco
Sweet smell of success

Venice has been a city of perfume-sellers since medieval times and it's to this tradition that the shop's name refers: the *muschieri* were the merchants who dealt in cosmetics, powders and scents. Owned by the Resta family since 1994, the shop is now managed by sisters Antonietta and Rosa, who took over in 2005 and shifted the business's focus to artistic perfume labels.

The room is packed with independent brands (strictly no big names) that the sisters have sourced from all over the world, as well as Italian scents by the likes of Gritti and Carthusia.
*1177 Calle Frezzeria, 30124
+39 041 522 8940*

Giuliana Longo, San Marco
Hats off

Located in the same shop since 1902, the Longo family sells hats to suit all styles. In her atelier upstairs, Giuliana Longo and her daughter-in-law make models for men and women that range from elaborate get-ups for Carnevale to the classic black berets that are favoured by gondoliers across the city in winter.

For a handsome sunshade pick up one of the panamas that Longo sources from Ecuador. Throw on the white, wide-brimmed Cuenca in summer to complete that quintessential Venetian look.
*4813 Calle del Lovo, 30124
+39 041 522 6454
giulianalongo.com*

Le Forcole, Dorsoduro
Oarsome work

Unless you own a gondola, you may not need one of Saverio Pastor's skilfully carved oars. The *fórcole* (oarlocks), however, are sculptural pieces that would look good in any living room.

Pastor (*pictured, left*) opened this workshop in 2002 and since 2004 has been training apprentice Pietro Meneghini (*pictured, above*). Together they carve these oddly shaped oar-rests from walnut or cherry trees. Each is manufactured with age-old traditional methods; stop by to see the pair at work with handsaws and hatchets.
*341 Fondamenta Soranzo, 30123
+39 041 522 5699
forcole.com*

Venice — Retail

⑦ Officine 904, Dorsoduro
Bags of choice

Paolo Porcu Rodriguez and Silvia Pavanello started bag brand Officine 904 in 2010 with just one item on their roster: the Market bag. Designed as a reinterpretation of the humble plastic bag, their first-born looked to clean architectural lines for inspiration. Since then the pair have stayed true to their pursuit of simplicity while also showing a penchant for vibrant colours.

Today the brand's permanent collection features 10 leather bag models available in a score of hues, all of them neatly arranged in rows of boxes that line the walls. Limited editions are released throughout the year to supplement the core range and there's also a collection of bracelets and foulards on offer.

2864 Calle Lunga San Barnaba, 30100
+39 041 524 2286
officine904.it

Cinematic creation

Roberta di Camerino's handbags are famous for being snapped on the arms of fashion icons such as Grace Kelly. Founded in 1945 by Giuliana Coen, the brand has made a name for itself with eccentric designs.
robertadicamerino.com

⑧ Fallani, Cannaregio
Handsome prints

A few steps from I Gesuiti (*see page 116*) is serigraphy workshop Fallani, set in an airy internal courtyard complete with a colonnade and a luminous glass ceiling.

Artists from Italy and beyond (including Renato Guttuso and Hans Richter) have come here to have their work printed by Fiorenzo Fallani, who started the venture in 1968. His sons now collaborate with international artists on limited-edition prints: bag one of these over Fallani's own slightly more predictable Venice-themed designs.

4875 Salizzada Seriman, 30121
+39 041 523 5772
fallanivenezia.com

⑨ Palwer, San Marco
Glittering prizes

After two decades working in Paris fashion houses (he was Emanuel Ungaro's creative director) Alessandro Palwer moved to Venice to found a jewellery brand in 2010. "Designing jewels was a liberation after creating clothes for so many years," he says. "I started drawing jewellery when I was very young: it was always a natural, spontaneous way of expressing myself."

Palwer's creations are inspired by sculptures and his travels. His chunkier models are statement pieces whereas the smooth, square rings are beautifully simple.
3151 Salizzada San Samuele, 30124
+ 39 041 528 5435
palwer.com

Ship shaper
Penzo also sells plans for a variety of vessels

⑩ Gilberto Penzo, San Polo
Modelling Venetian boats

Gilberto Penzo (*pictured*) is keeping the Venetian boatmaking heritage alive in miniature. His intricate models of traditional and modern boats alike, from the elegant gondola to the trusty vaporetto, are all handmade in his San Polo workshop.

Penzo's family built boats so the skills are very much in his blood. "I want to bring dignity to a world seen, at best, as a folkloristic backdrop," he says. "My objective is to save the last traditional boats and the memory of the techniques used to make them."
2681 Calle Seconda dei Saoneri, 30125
+ 39 041 524 6139
veniceboats.com

Venice Retail

Opticians
See and be seen

①
L'Altra Ottica, Castello and San Polo
Specs-tacular range

All the glasses in L'Altra Ottica's in-house line begin life with artisans in the mountainous Cadore area, near Italy's capital of specs-making, Belluno. The shop's founder Matteo Vianello and optician Massimo Zane often travel to the mainland factory just to make sure production is running smoothly.
 Most of their designs are made from celluloid but the shop also stocks external brands made from wood or metal: on the shelves of both of the small chain's locations (the original shop in Castello, founded in 2007, and the second in San Polo) you'll spot smart options by international hitters such as Moscot, IC Berlin and Mykita.
6206 Calle Lunga Santa Maria Formosa, 30100; 1239 Calle de Mezzo, 30125
+39 041 241 1856;
+39 041 520 1099
laltraottica.com

②
Ottica Urbani, San Marco
Eye-class products

This bijou shop close to Piazza San Marco has sold fanciful eyewear since the 1950s and is popular with the design-conscious. Architects Carlo Scarpa and Le Corbusier were clients, the latter ordering the Tondo model that has today been elaborated with Murano glass lenses.
 The shop stocks cutting-edge labels, as well as an in-house collection of designs produced by craftsmen in the eyewear district around Belluno using unique materials for the frames: think water-buffalo horn, wood and steel.
1280 Bocca de Piazza, 30124
+39 041 522 4140
otticaurbani.com

③
Micromega, San Marco
Light, fantastic

Fancy a pair of glasses with leaf-shaped lenses or sprigs for frames? At Micromega almost anything is possible (including tamer options). "The only limit is the imagination," says founder Roberto Carlon.
 Whether rimmed with titanium or gold, all frames are remarkably thin: the brand was born in 2000 when Carlon patented his "one-gram" ultra-light technology. The prototypes inside the shop are only for inspiration: all frames are customised to designs by Carlon and his son Ugo and assembled at the brand's Venice laboratory.
2436 Calle delle Ostreghe, 30124
+39 041 296 0765
micromegaottica.com

Bookshops
Bounty for bibliophiles

Self published
Bruno stocks about 1,000 titles on its shelves

①
Bruno with Motto, Dorsoduro
Small press titles

Since 2011, Andrea Codolo and colleague Giacomo Covacich have been working together as graphic designers and creating the branding for many Venetian cultural institutions. Then in 2013 their studio started a new chapter: making and selling books.
 Art and design titles lie alongside obscureced fanzines and architecture books produced and printed in their backroom office. "The shop is a chance to show off books that combine interesting graphic design, great content and quality of print," says Covacich.
2729 Calle Lunga San Barnaba, 30123
+39 041 523 0737
b-r-u-n-o.it

060

Venice — Retail

③
Cafoscarina, Dorsoduro
Novel approach

Born as the official book outlet of the Università Ca' Foscari, this shop now has three locations. While the original in Cannaregio still caters to the business faculty nearby, compact Cafoscarina 3 in Dorsoduro packs an abundant selection of travel and English-language titles and is your best bet if you want to pick up the latest novel in its original language.
  This branch focuses on Asian studies too. A short hop across the small *campo* will lead you to the biggest branch, which is filled to the brim with arts and humanities titles.
3259 Calle Foscari, 30100
+39 041 240 4803
cafoscarina.it

②
Libreria Acqua Alta, Castello
Volumes of water

This extraordinary canal-level bookshop occasionally gets flooded in winter. Rather than fight it, owner Luigi Frizzo peacefully coexists with high water by stacking the good books (new and used, in many languages) in bathtubs, which in turn stand on books (some are inside boats, including a gondola). Books even form a sturdy staircase on the outdoor terrace.
  If you're not into books then visit just to enjoy the nautical memorabilia, such as ship's wheels and wooden barrels sawn in half – not to mention the atmosphere of genial chaos.
Campiello del Tintor, 30122
+39 041 296 0841

④
Libreria Cluva, Santa Croce
Architecture and more

It may be set inside the Università Iuav di Venezia – beyond its Carlo Scarpa-designed doorway (*see page 106*) – but this bookshop's remit goes well beyond the course's reading list.
  Since it was founded in 1962 the bookshop's main focus has been architecture – but today its titles span everything from urbanism to fashion. Owners Patrizia Zamparo and husband Angelo offer savvy guidance. In 2011 they started their own publishing house, which brings out titles on Venice as well as academic treaties.
191 Fondamenta dei Tolentini, 30135
+39 041 522 6910
libreriacluva.com

What? How else did you think owls got so wise?

Things we'd buy
―― Shop talk

Venice has long catered to visitors with a passion for purchasing and money to burn. The city was built on commerce and trade; those wily Venetians even converted their most famous bridge into a shopping arcade in the 1400s.

Although today's travellers are more likely to leave with pockets stuffed with cheap trinkets and soulless souvenirs than silk and spices, there's more to the city's retail offering than masks and Murano glass (although we will, of course, show you where to source the finest of both).

A clutch of independent designers and makers scattered throughout the city are quietly turning out quality items as they have done for generations: the trick is finding them among the carnival of cheap imitators and tacky tourist traps. Well, you need look no further.

From brogues and boats to biscuits and booze, you'll want to save a spot in your suitcase for these alternative keepsakes. And not a sequin or feather in sight.

Venice
Things we'd buy

01 Jacket by Barena
barenavenezia.com
02 Mask by Ca' Macana
camacana.com
03 Coffee by Torrefazione Cannaregio
torrefazionecannaregio.it
04 Anchovy paste by Orco
orco.it
05 Small Caps poster from Bragorà
bragora.it
06 Colussi Baicoli biscuits from Pasticceria Tonolo
colussi.net
07 Erminio Scortegagna wooden kitchenware from Madera
maderavenezia.it
08 Pasta by Sgambaro
sgambaro.com
09 *Venice: A Document* by Sara Marini and Alberto Bertagna from Bruno
b-r-u-n-o.it
10 Vase by Carlo Moretti
lisola.com
11 Ferrari Brut by Ferrari
ferraritrento.it
12 Inama wine from Cantine del Vino già Schiavi
cantinaschiavi.com
13 Grappa by Nardini
nardini.it
14 *Invisible Cities* by Italo Calvino from Cafoscarina
cafoscarina.it
15 Gondolier hat by Giuliana Longo
giulianalongo.com
16 Spinning tops by Angelo Dalla Venezia
+39 041 721 659
17 Sunglasses by Ottica Urbani
otticaurbani.com
18 Gondolier shirts by Emilio Ceccato
emilioceccato.com
19 Furlane by Pied à Terre
piedaterre-venice.com
20 Zip pouches by Inzu
in-zu.it
21 Wooden-boat kits by Gilberto Penzo
veniceboats.com
22 Brogues by Daniela Ghezzo
danielaghezzo.it

Venice
Things we'd buy

01 Chinos by Incotex
slowear.com
02 Extra-virgin olive oil by JW Marriott Venice
jwvenice.com
03 Perfume by The Merchant of Venice
themerchantofvenice.net
04 *Carlo Scarpa's Tomba Brion* by Guido Guidi from Libreria Cluva
libreriacluva.com
05 Notebooks by Alberto Valese
albertovalese-ebru.it
06 *Carlo Scarpa & Tobia Scarpa: Dialogo Sospeso* from Cafoscarina
cafoscarina.it
07 Lido swimwear by Al Duca D'Aosta
alducadaosta.com
08 Wallet and bag by Declare
dclr.it
09 Wine by Venissa
venissa.it
10 EX B beer by Spazio Punch
spaziopunch.com

12 essays
—— Venice explored

①
A most noble and singular city
The history of Venice
by Alex Bamji,
historian

②
Best food bar none
Eating like a Venetian
Russell Norman,
restaurateur

③
Sink or swim?
Model tourist
Megan Gibson,
Monocle

④
Garden variety
Venetian horticulture
Jenny Condie,
writer

⑤
Latent Orient
Eastern inspirations
Chloë Ashby,
Monocle

⑥
I spy
Venetian voyeurism
James Taylor-Foster,
writer

⑦
Routes/canals
Navigating the city
Ivan Carvalho,
Monocle

⑧
Taking a punt
Life as a gondolier
Gino Macropodio,
gondolier

⑨
The biennale
A guide for the uninitiated
Aaron Betsky,
curator

⑩
Water world
Tides of change
Chiara Rimella,
Monocle

⑪
Identity crisis
Masks in Venetian society
Laura Morelli,
art historian

⑫
Get a room
Overnight stays
Francesca Bortolotto Possati,
hotelier

Perhaps not the most peaceful place to read...

ESSAY 01

A most noble and singular city
The history of Venice

From origins as murky as canal water, Venice established a reputation as a hub of Mediterranean trade and power.

by Alex Bamji, historian

The first guide to Venice was published in 1581. On the title page of *Venice, Most Noble and Singular City*, Francesco Sansovino summarised what – even then – made the city so special: past wars, successful due to the participation of the city's rulers; the lives of the doges and Venetian writers; the churches, buildings and palaces rising out of the lagoon; and the laws and customs. Sansovino's promotion of the superiority of Venetian politics, culture and society was neither the first nor last contribution to the "myth of Venice": the idea that it was "singular" or unique. Proponents argued that the city's distinctive origins, lagoon setting, mix of people, and political and social structure fostered stability, justice and liberty – and assured independence and longevity.

The city's origins are uncertain. It was founded in 421, 452 or 568, depending on your source, but chroniclers at least agree that the earliest Venetians were refugees from an influx of heathen barbarians on the mainland.

From the outset the settlers had divine protection, cemented in 828 when the relics of Saint Mark the Evangelist were transferred to Venice from Alexandria, smuggled out under a layer of pork. The city's political system took shape from 697, when the first doge was elected as highest official. The Venetian republic endured until 1797 when the Great Council, faced with massing Napoleonic troops on the mainland, voted itself out of existence.

> "Power came as much from Venice's ability to take advantage of external circumstances as from its internal strength"

Advocates of Venice's greatness hailed its mixed constitution, which mirrored ancient Rome in combining democracy (the Great Council, of which all adult male nobles were members), aristocracy (an elected Senate that formulated domestic and foreign policy) and monarchy (the doge). Membership of the nobility was closed to new families in 1297 but the middle social group of "citizens" gained power through roles in the civil service and devotional confraternities. The artisans, fishermen and servants who made up the *popolani* (lower orders) had little inclination to rebel, perhaps valuing the chances of working in a bustling port or appreciating – in the case of the shipbuilders – the provision of five litres of wine per worker per day.

Venice's detractors argued that its stability came through repression. The Council of Ten upheld state security; established in 1310 and described by one 16th-century noble as a "very terrifying magistracy", it had spies eavesdrop on seditious conversations in the pharmacies and barbershops that were the sociable coffeehouses of their day. Suspects were suspended from the ceiling of the Council's chamber in the heart of the Palazzo Ducale to elicit confessions and traitors were executed between the columns of the Piazzetta. Workers could report neighbours for tax evasion or breaking public health laws by slipping a denunciation into boxes fronted with a scowling face or the mouth of a lion.

Power came as much from Venice's ability to take advantage of external circumstances as from its internal strength. Its medieval rulers exploited the decline of Byzantium to build an empire, first along the Adriatic coast and in the Mediterranean, then on the mainland around the city. As the centre of east-west shipping routes, Venice gained prosperity from the trade in spices, sugar and silk. The people who accompanied the goods made the city a melting pot of cultures, languages and religions.

As global trade shifted to the Atlantic, Venice turned inwards. But the decadence of Carnevale, courtesans and coffeehouses came with ever-growing numbers of visitors and cultural vibrancy. Venice pioneered public opera with extravagant sets, special effects and tickets affordable to all.

In the 21st century, Venice is still shaped by its interactions with the outside world, whether the periodic incursions of art and artists for the biennale or the foreign investment that transforms crumbling palaces into hotels and retail emporia. As Venice persists in adapting to the world around it, it remains a most noble and singular city. — (M)

Venetian firsts

01 Patents
Europe's earliest patent system was put in place in 1474.
02 Ghettos
In 1516 the world's first Jewish ghetto was established.
03 Public opera houses
Teatro San Cassiano opened in 1637.

ABOUT THE WRITER: Alex Bamji is a historian who divides her time between her students at the University of Leeds and her research into the history of death in the dusty state archives of Venice.

Venice Essays

ESSAY 02
Best food bar none
Eating like a Venetian

Looking for the tastiest meals in Venice? It's not the restaurants you need to be checking out. Dive off the main drag and into the narrow backstreets to discover the best kitchens that the city has to offer.

by Russell Norman, restaurateur

Venice is a city of extremes. As anyone who has visited in the stifling heat of summer will testify, it is sticky, smelly and teeming with tourists. Yet come winter the icy Dolomite winds turn Venice into a fridge, the eerily empty streets making the place feel like a cemetery. However, whatever the weather and no matter how harsh the conditions, Venice somehow manages to seduce you completely, convincing you that you are in the greatest city on the planet: magical, beautiful and majestically poised above the waves.

The contrast between land and sea is at the heart of the city's identity crisis too. Here is an ancient settlement built over the course of 1,500 years on marshy mud in a vast lagoon that straddles the threshold between two domains: estranged from mainland Italy but punished by the waters that initially afforded it protection.

And in modern-day Venice another contradiction confounds me with every visit: for a city that has such proud culinary traditions, its restaurants are, with a handful of notable exceptions, universally terrible.

The oddest of all its discrepancies, however, is that while the ghastly grub found in the tourist traps around Piazza San Marco and the Ponte di Rialto is shockingly expensive, the best food in Venice is actually as cheap as chips. There is a baffling inverse relationship between the amount of money you pay for food and its quality. And this is because the real deal isn't found in the city's restaurants but in its wine bars.

In Venice they call these bars *bàcari* (*see pages 31 to 35*). That's a Venetian word to describe humble establishments, often with standing room only, serving *ombre* (small glasses of young, local wine) and *cichèti* (inexpensive tasty snacks). While you may prefer to relax in the evening with a seafood supper at a decent restaurant (and yes, there are a few: my current favourites are Antiche Carampane, Osteria Alle Testiere, Paradiso Perduto and Al Covo) there is only one way to eat during the day – and that is at a *bàcaro*. Furthermore you will often find that specific places

---

Venetian bàcari

01 Al Mercà, San Polo
Try the tuna-and-horseradish roll and a Campari spritz.
02 La Cantina, Cannaregio
For excellent sashimi and its own-label beer, Morgana.
03 Cà' d'Oro Alla Vedova, Cannaregio
Stand at the bar with a glass of wine.

have individual specialities that make them worth the journey, so it's sometimes sensible to plan a bar crawl to take in a few *bàcari* in a single afternoon.

My first port of call when I arrive in Venice is usually All'Arco, a family-run postage-stamp-sized snack bar that punches well above its weight in culinary terms. Francesco and his son Matteo look after the food, while mum Anna takes care of the wine. I recommend you simply ask Matteo to choose what's good from the nearby Rialto market that morning and make you one of his fantastic specials. I always drink the delicious prosecco col fondo: natural, cloudy and on the lees.

Across town in Dorsoduro, situated on a pretty canal behind the Gallerie dell'Accademia, is Cantine del Vino già Schiavi. Probably the most famous *bàcaro* in Venice, and cunningly disguised as a wine shop, it's a must-visit. Say hello to Alessandra, the matriarch who makes all the *cichèti* and raised the strapping lads serving you from behind the bar.

This is the best way I know to eat like a Venetian – and don't worry about finding your appetite. Something miraculous happens when you start to eat this way: you actually get hungrier. As they say in Italian: *l'appetito vien mangiando*. — (M)

> "There is a baffling inverse relationship between the amount of money you pay for food and its quality"

ABOUT THE WRITER: Russell Norman is an award-winning restaurateur, broadcaster and food writer. His third book, *My Venetian Kitchen*, will be published in 2018.

Venice Essays

ESSAY 03

Sink or swim?
Model tourist

Venice has an uneasy relationship with tourism, especially when it comes chugging along in the form of a whopping cruise ship. As such, it's vital that visitors make a good impression.

by Megan Gibson, Monocle

The fact that Venice is sinking is something of a siren song for people from all parts of the world wanting to visit its grand palazzos and cruise its canals while they still can. Yet upon arrival it can be hard to ignore the elephant (or, perhaps, hippo) in the lagoon: in the eyes of some Venetians it's these visitors who are hastening the city's downfall.

Just as Rome wasn't built in a day, neither was Venice's fraught relationship with tourism, the very industry that keeps it financially afloat. (Back in the 1950s the writer Mary McCarthy wrote that there is "no use pretending that the tourist Venice is not the real Venice".) And while there are

Venice Essays

How to be a model tourist

01 Respect the waiting area
At vaporetto stops, that yellow line is there for a reason.
02 Don't feed the birds
As well as the risk of pigeon poo, it may result in a fine.
03 Put it away
The warm weather is no excuse to bare your chest.

several cities that struggle with their designation as a destination, the residents in the likes of Barcelona, Paris and Amsterdam seem to regard tourism with a resigned curmudgeonliness.

In Venice it's a different story. More than 20 million visitors arrive every year and most days in the high season see a near doubling of the population on account of day-trippers. As a result some Venetians are unable to mask their disdain for out-of-towners, glowering at anyone with a foreign accent.

First-timers can be forgiven for being taken aback when encountering a scowl; "What have I done, I've only just arrived?" Try not to take it personally. The real bugbear for Venetians is the cruise industry, thanks to massive ships churning up the Canale della Giudecca before disgorging tens of thousands of tourists who crowd the city's squares and alleyways and line up on the Ponte di Rialto in order to take selfies in the sunshine. Their biggest sin, however, is the fact that they abscond back to their ship come early evening, without so much as buying a meal, and head off to the next port. Their contribution to the local economy is negligible and in their wake they leave a mess and a bad impression.

The tension between Venetians and the cruise industry has boiled over several times in recent years. Protesters have been known to block the Canale della Giudecca, where liners try to navigate from the Adriatic, using anything from boats to their own bodies bobbing in the water. Look up from the city centre's narrower canals and you'll see protest flags bearing a cruise ship and an angry red "No" sign fluttering from many windows.

"Ask any Venetian about the best part of their city and their scowl will swiftly fade"

While the local government has attempted to grapple with the growing anger at the cruise industry, many Venetians are frustrated with the lack of progress they've made. A ban on large ships entering the city centre in 2014 was overturned after just three months as a result of pressure from the cruise industry.

While this resistance is understandable, it can make for some uncomfortable encounters – particularly, it seems, for Americans or the American-sounding (my Canadian accent does me no favours). So what makes for a model visitor?

First, it's important to keep in mind that those who complain about day-trippers hurting Venice don't believe that the city isn't worth exploring: they protest out of love for their home. Ask any Venetian about the best part of their city and their scowl will swiftly fade as they pour forth advice and ideas for hidden corners to discover and experience. It was by asking a reticent local for recommendations of what to see and do on Giudecca that I learned of all the exciting artist studios that exist on the island (*see page 136*). Similarly, if you can stomach talking politics in between bites of *cichèti*, ask a Venetian for their thoughts on the cruise industry – everyone has an opinion on the issue and discussing it with a resident is often rather enlightening.

And if you still find yourself the recipient of a glower here or there? Chalk it up as a part of the city's character and continue to marvel at the sights. — (M)

ABOUT THE WRITER: MONOCLE's senior editor Megan Gibson has been with the magazine since 2015. She considers herself a model visitor and will forgive you for mistaking her for an American.

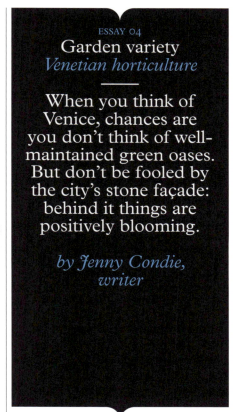

ESSAY 04
Garden variety
Venetian horticulture

When you think of Venice, chances are you don't think of well-maintained green oases. But don't be fooled by the city's stone façade: behind it things are positively blooming.

by Jenny Condie, writer

From the everyday bustle of the Rialto market to the sublimity of a Bellini altarpiece, Venice's treasures are arrayed like polished wares along a well-trodden *calle*. Masked revellers posing on a picturesque bridge? Check. A gondola floating down a shimmering canal? Check. It's both just as you'd expect and a glorious surprise.

At first it might not appear that there is anything missing but sooner or later our senses are awoken by the echoing warble of a blackbird, the enticing waft of a floral scent or the glimpse of a groping tendril of wisteria creeping over a high wall, and we realise that this city of stone and brick is concealing something from us.

Venice Essays

There are more than 500 gardens nestling among the tightly packed houses and palazzos – a smattering of green in the terracotta mosaic of the cityscape. Visitors have been remarking on the improbable nature of their existence for hundreds of years, amazed at the ability of plants and even large trees to thrive in such saline conditions, and awed by the size of some of the plots and the botanical variety that they contain.

A seagoing people anchored to a few acres of shifting mudflats in an exposed lagoon, the Venetians have always hugely valued what little soil they could wrest from the tides. Their houses were set among vegetable plots and orchards. Now paved over, these *campi* (fields) still exist, only now they ring with the shouts of playing children, the tramp of tourists and the clink of wine glasses. As the city ran out of space for building, the larger private gardens were swallowed up and smallholders moved out of the centre to the various islands dotted around the lagoon, although not too far: vineyards and olive groves can still be found within earshot of the bells of Basilica di San Marco if you know where to look.

Of the numerous monastery gardens that once provided food and medicinal herbs for Venice's religious orders, a few survive – and with pre-planning, some may even be visited. These are not tourist sites but places of prayer and work. Palladio's austere Chiesa del Santissimo Redentore on Giudecca is attended by the Capuchin Friars, who also run a soup kitchen. Visitors may be admitted upon request for a short tour of the garden that supplies the kitchens.

On the other side of the city, the monks of the Discalced Carmelite Order once

Venetian gardens

01 Chiesa degli Scalzi
Ponder the mystical and symbolic significance.
02 Giardini Savorgnan
A Venetian baron's English dream.
03 Palazzo Soranzo Cappello
Home and artistically shabby garden of the fictional Misses Bordereau.

> "The Venetians have always hugely valued what little soil they could wrest from the tides"

specialised in the production of lemon-balm water and had fields of perfumed *Melissa moldavica* stretching all the way to the northern lagoon shore. Half of their land disappeared under train tracks with the building of a railway but they are still there, their Garden of Contemplation separated from the noisy platforms by a high wall. Little bottles of refreshing Acqua di Melissa are still sold in their shop on site and the monastery garden is open to the public from time to time.

Medieval Venice's monopoly of the lucrative spice trade elicited a near-obsession with plants and the substances derived from them. Private herb gardens sprouted up all over the city in a pursuit of knowledge that received the stamp of officialdom with the 1543 founding of the first botanical garden in nearby Padua. The city's apothecaries, whose eccentric remedies included the famous Teriaca (containing viper flesh), were renowned throughout Europe and strictly supervised by the ever-watchful Venetian authorities. Less exotic but certainly more sweet-smelling potions can today be acquired from the inmates of the Venetian women's prison, who market their own line of beauty products – Rio Terà dei Pensieri – from herbs grown and distilled in the prison garden.

Glimpses of more carefree garden pleasures are evident in the writings of Casanova and the paintings of Francesco Guardi but echoes of those 18th-century delights can be hard to find. As every

ESSAY 05
Latent Orient
Eastern inspirations

Venice's trade relationship with Byzantium and Cairo brought silk, spices and a melange of exotic cultural influences you can still see today – if you know where to look.

by Chloë Ashby, Monocle

A turbaned character, hobbling on one leg, pauses to urge on his pack animal. Behind him, caught mid-stride with one foreleg raised, is his bridled camel carrying a bulky load. This charming 14th-century stone bas-relief on the façade of the Palazzo Mastelli in Cannaregio is one of many nods to the East that you'll find in this beguiling city.

Ever since it was founded in the 5th century, Venice has relied on fishing and trade, and the latter – thanks to its advantageous position on shipping routes – led to the East. Through traders, artisans and material goods the city absorbed a wealth of visual ideas – and as a result of this outward-looking perspective, it flourished. Venice is

neglectful gardener knows, yesterday's Eden is today's impenetrable thicket. One such languishing garden has been sensitively restored to recall its role in inspiring Henry James's brilliant 1888 novella *The Aspern Papers*. Its rambling roses and jasmine frequently form a romantically dishevelled backdrop for artworks during the biennale. Another is the garden of Ca' Zenobio degli Armeni, situated in a melancholy and beautiful corner of Dorsoduro. The sumptuously decorated ballroom on the first floor looks out over a garden that preserves intact a temple-like *casino* (little house), the weekend cottage of its time, in this case built to house a library but notoriously resorted for more amorous pursuits.

Tastes changed with the end of the Venetian republic in 1797. Along with the new democratic ideals brought by Napoleon came a penchant for landscape gardening – a tall order in an enclosed space on flat terrain in the middle of a populous city. But that didn't stop some of the richer nobles from trying. One of the grandest survivors of this tendency, the Giardini Savorgnan, is now a public park a stone's throw from one of the city's busiest thoroughfares; few visitors trailing their suitcases along the Lista di Spagna could suspect the existence of its green and leafy bowers.

The invading French were responsible for creating the public gardens at the far east of the city that now house the biennale pavilions. From here the views out over the south lagoon and west towards San Marco are incomparable. On a hot day the trickle of the water fountain, the shade of the plane trees and the forlorn sculptures poking out of unkempt bushes are the perfect antidote to mass-tourism madness. — (M)

ABOUT THE WRITER: Jenny Condie is a failed gardener who has lived in Venice for some years, writing, teaching and yearning for a garden. She is the author of *The Gardens of Venice and the Veneto*.

Venice Essays

> **Eastern attractions**
>
> **01 Basilica di San Pietro di Castello**
> The Campanile pays homage to the Lighthouse of Alexandria.
> **02 Ca' Dario**
> Adopted a marble "telephone-dial" motif from Cairo.
> **03 Basilica di San Marco**
> Shaped like the Holy Apostles in Constantinople.

inextricably bound to the Orient through myth, commerce, architecture and art, and the traces of that connection are everywhere.

Stroll through the city's labyrinthine centre and you'll soon feel the presence of the East. As you weave between densely built-up apartment buildings and parishes you'll turn down countless crooked *calli*, crossing a wooden bridge here and reaching nothing but a silky canal there. To your left a dazzling palazzo is topped with gap-toothed crenellations, while to your right stray greenery hints at a walled garden. As you stumble upon an open piazza your senses are awakened by the sounds and smells of a colourful outdoor market, reminiscent of a souk.

Venice has long been compared to eastern mercantile centres and no wonder: located off the northeastern coast of Italy in the Adriatic Sea, between Rome and Byzantium, for a time it was Europe's gateway to the Orient. By the 13th century it was the primary port for spices bound for western and northern Europe, and stocked precious textiles from lands beyond the Levant. This continued in defiance of the Papacy, which objected to a Christian city dealing with Muslim rulers. Two cities it interacted with were Byzantine Constantinople and Islamic Cairo; the visual imagery of both can be seen in Venice's art and architecture.

Even its founding myth is rooted in the East: in 828, two Venetian merchants swiped the bones of Saint Mark, the city's patron saint, from a tomb in Alexandria and brought them home in a boat bundled up with some pork. The Basilica di San Marco was built to house the relics and the story of the *translatio* (their acquisition and transportation) is told in gilt mosaics on its west façade. In the semi-dome above the portal on the far left is the only surviving 13th-century original: the processional transfer into the church of the open casket holding the splendidly dressed body of the saint.

The mosaic and its story establishes the city as an authorised player in the eastern Mediterranean. Venice's founding myth is tied up with the city's capability to move material goods from one place to another; as well as providing the city with a sense of origins, it gave a nod of approval to the practice of appropriation that lay at the root of Venetian existence.

The decorative shell of the basilica is plastered with eastern booty, most of which was brought back from Constantinople after

Venice sacked it in 1204. The quadriga of bronze horses on the second-storey terrace (now a copy), the exotic marble columns around the portals, and the richly carved bas-reliefs are all material testimony to Venetian exploits overseas.

"Venice is inextricably bound to the Orient through myth, commerce, architecture and art, and the traces of that connection are everywhere"

It's no surprise that Piazza San Marco – the centre of religious and political life – is also the glorified dumping ground for these spoils. But not all the eastern trappings in Venice were pilfered: some were borrowed ideas. Just as the gold-backed mosaics on the basilica were inspired by an art refined in eastern Christendom and brought to Venice by Byzantine craftsmen, the architecture in the piazza was influenced by that in the East. The tall cupolas on the basilica recall the mosques in Cairo, while the marble grilles on its windows were modelled on those in Damascus. Similarly the pink-and-white lozenge pattern on the façade of the Palazzo Ducale echoes mosques Venetian merchants would have seen along the Silk Road in Asia.

Those merchants also copied eastern motifs on their palazzos, to advertise their trading success. The Ca' d'Oro on the Canal Grande was lavishly decorated by its owner Marino Contarini with Islamic-esque multi-lobed arches, lacy arabesque traceries and slender Egyptian-style pinnacles; as its name implies, the Golden House was also originally painted in gold leaf like a Persian palace.

Back in Cannaregio, near the camel relief, three turbaned Moors and their weighed-down servant occupy the Campo dei Mori. These figures, carved in Istrian stone, represent the three Mastelli brothers, silk merchants who came to Venice from Greece in 1112 and lived in the Palazzo Mastelli. One guards the former house of great Venetian painter Jacopo Tintoretto, himself the son of a silk dyer.

By aligning itself with the East, Venice confirmed its national and cultural singularity in relation to neighbouring cities in the West. Today, with swathes of tourists and international cultural events such as the biennale, it continues to welcome unexpected minglings. As in the medieval world, Venetian identity remains tightly bound to distant lands through culture and commerce. The result? A hallucinatory world that is so much more than merely Italian. — (M)

ABOUT THE WRITER: As editor of this guide, Chloë Ashby enjoyed finding and losing her way through Venice's *calli*. A graduate of the Courtauld Institute of Art, she spent her final year studying the cross-cultural exchange between Venice and Byzantium.

ESSAY 06
I spy
Venetian voyeurism

It's easy to spot the true Venetians among the tourists, so long as you know who's watching who. Here's an expat's advice on working the city – and its crowd.

by James Taylor-Foster, writer

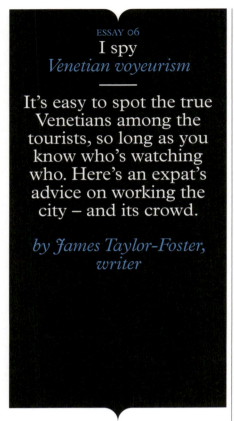

Believe it or not, Venice is a place in which people actually live. Take the time to look and you'll notice the same characters walking their dogs or taking *caffè* and *pizzetti* each morning.

How do you spot them? It depends on the season. In winter, when the lagoon is often shrouded by thick fog, *veneziane* of a certain age might be weighed down by furs – handed down through generations – or perhaps an ankle-length cape. As the day sinks into Venice's unique inky-black night they, like gleaming gondolas, glide quietly through the city. In the summer months, when the intense heat and humidity make *acqua frizzante* on ice or prosecco (which tends to flow like water here) the only viable drinking options, the

gente per bene – the "true" Venetians – always appear nonchalant, even if they're wrapped in brightly coloured silks.

Venice is a city of voyeurs; a place in which being seen and looking at others should be at the top of your agenda. Spend more than a few days here and you're likely to have taken up this sport regardless of your intentions. Incalculable numbers of tourists have returned home lumbered by purchases that seem sensible in the moment but, when reassessed in the cold light of day, appear rather decadent: new spectacles, for example (the city's *ottiche* are famous for their fantastical designs), faux furs or a pair of trousers two sizes too small. All fine for getting noticed in Venice; back home, not so much.

Ambling down the Strada Nova – the longest stretch of street that you will find on the central islands of the city – is about exchanging glances with passers-by: twitching an eyebrow or creasing a smile. In a city in which you are unable to rush even if you try desperately to arrive somewhere on time, residents make peace with a slower pace of life. At times it feels as though the world spins slower in Venice – these are, after all, no ordinary *calli* or *sotopòrteghi* (covered passageways). A meandering walk through San Marco, San Polo or Dorsoduro is an experience unique and unforgettable.

"Venice is a city of voyeurs; a place in which being seen and looking at others should be at the top of your agenda"

Perhaps the best way to think about Venice is as an interior: a huge living room (Piazza San Marco was described by Napoleon as "the drawing room of Europe"), dining room and terrace all rolled into one. The *campi*, the Venetian take on a piazza, are places to while away the day. At the height of summer, groups of friends will migrate to a single *campo* following the path of the

Venice
Essays

Watch this space

01 Campo San Giacomo dell'Orio
Pick up a pastry from Majer and settle in the square.
02 Campo di Sant'Agnese
Find a spot of shade beneath trees – a rare treat.
03 Campo Santa Maria Nova
Watch gondolas glide by Santa Maria dei Miracoli.

ESSAY 07

Routes/canals
Navigating the city

The labyrinthine alleys of Venice can be a nightmare to negotiate – but paying attention to the city's street signs can give you more than just simple directions.

by Ivan Carvalho, Monocle

sun. While older people share gossip and a cigarette, young children play with coloured chalk or kick around a ball – all against the backdrop of some of the most spectacular and historically charged architecture in Europe. In Campo Santa Margherita, strategically positioned between the city's two great scholarly institutions, the average age of the revellers drops to about 25. If you're out after midnight, this is the place to be.

Aside from these quotidian rituals, Venice is a city of grand ceremony: annual festivals of celebration and gratitude (such as the Festa del Redentore or the Festa della Madonna della Salute), prowess and civic might (such as the Festa della Sensa, in which the doge, nowadays the incumbent mayor, weds the city to the sea as indissolubly one) and Carnevale are performed with the utmost sincerity. While these can be outwardly read as rather garish tourist traps there continues, beneath the superficial costume, a sacred tradition among locals. In spite of wider trends, Venice continues to be home to a profoundly religious people – one of the dwindling threads that maintains the city's soul and vibrancy. — (M)

Visitors to Venice face a navigational nightmare. In the past, those who were confused by the lagoon city's twisting maze of alleys could be seen gripping unwieldy fold-out maps as they attempted to get their bearings. Nowadays they stand out for having their heads down, glued to the maps on their mobile phones and putting themselves at risk of a tumble into a canal or a stumble down the steps of one of the hundreds of bridges that dot the cityscape.

Those willing to look up from their screens will soon find a simpler, more informative way to navigate Venice. *Nizioleti*, Venetian dialect for "little sheets", are the

ABOUT THE WRITER: James Taylor-Foster is a writer, designer and broadcaster in the fields of architecture and urbanism. He co-curated the Nordic Pavilion at the 15th Biennale Architettura and moved to Venice in 2016.

077

Venice Essays

Street smarts

01 Rio Terà
Denotes a street built over an old canal.
02 Ramo
A short street that often dead-ends.
03 Ponte dei Pugni
A bridge where two working-class factions used to fight.

whitewashed rectangular street signs that can be found adorning the sides of ageing palazzos throughout the watery metropolis (*see page 121*). They were introduced in the early 19th century, when Napoleon's forces occupied the territory and needed a way to make sense of the labyrinth of streets that they now controlled.

A glance at the names Venetians use to identify certain areas and structures allows one to delve into the city's rich history. Often families, who were noble or noted for some special reason and inhabited a nearby address, lent their name to the likes of a square or bridge. The Ponte delle Meraviglie (Bridge of Marvels) derives its name from a story about a family who lived in front of the bridge and whose ugly-duckling daughter was miraculously transformed into a great beauty one evening. Other names were taken from businesses that were based at certain addresses: there are streets dedicated to trades, ranging from blacksmiths to lawyers. And then there are names of nationalities that were linked to specific neighbourhoods when the city was a prominent trading outpost, such as Castello's Ponte dei Greci (Bridge of the Greeks).

Stencilled directly onto the sides of buildings in black enamel on bright-white plaster, there are some 4,000 *nizioleti* scattered across Venice and they are in constant need of upkeep. "The humidity in Venice takes its toll on them," says architect Denis Tommasin, who works at Area Restauro, the firm tasked by city hall to restore the signs. Workers paint each letter by hand with the aid of steel cutouts of the alphabet in Bodoni, the typeface that has become the official font of the *nizioleti*.

"A glance at the names Venetians use to identify certain areas and structures allows one to delve into the city's rich history"

Names are usually expressed in Venetian although one city councillor attempted to promote the Italian spelling of words, a move that provoked ire. In place of *via* and *piazza*, passers-by see *calle* and *campo*, with each painted in a specific character size. "Residents are very fond of the *nizioleti*," says Tommasin. "They're part of the city's identity

– just like black cabs in London. They make Venice unique." The old-fashioned markers typically appear at the beginning and end of a street, though given the numerous intersecting pedestrian lanes in the city Tommasin admits that this set-up doesn't always make life easy for those trying to direct either themselves or others. Another difficulty is the fact that some street names are duplicated across the various *sestieri* of Venice: you'll find a street called Malvasia in both Castello and Cannaregio.

Even residents themselves have a hard time remembering every nook and corner and at times will point people in the right direction of a destination by signalling the presence of a butcher's shop or bar. Still, Tommasin wouldn't have it any other way. "The beauty of these *nizioleti* is that behind many there lies a history lesson," he says. "It's more than a means to find your way around: it's a means to find out about the city's past." — (M)

ABOUT THE WRITER: Since 2007 Ivan Carvalho has been the Milan correspondent of MONOCLE magazine. He prefers visiting Venice and its many *bàcari* in winter when the city is cloaked in fog and mostly free of crowds.

ESSAY 08
Taking a punt
Life as a gondolier

As they ply their trade on the canals, they're one of the most recognisable symbols of Venice. But the gondoliers are so much more than boatmen: they're the eyes and ears of the city.

by Gino Macropodio, gondolier, as told to Beatrice Carmi

I come from a time when children, after learning how to talk and walk, learned how to swim and row. When the world moved at an oar's pace, rather than at motor speed. I was born in 1930 into a family of gondoliers: my father was one, as was my grandfather and my great-grandfather before him. It was a profession handed down from one generation to the next. My father taught me how to row and when I turned 18, the minimum age required, I officially became a gondolier.

The work season was only during the summer. It started at Easter and finished in September, after which the city was deserted. For the rest of the year I did

5 E Venice Essays

what I pleased. I travelled a lot, to places such as Paris and the US. I was a bachelor so I went wherever the wind took me. In 1955 I visited London for the screening of *Summertime*, a film with Katharine Hepburn and Rossano Brazzi that was shot in Venice. Plot aside I think it's the most beautiful film about Venice to date. It portrays its golden age and does the city justice.

> "The gondolier used to be a sort of cicerone: he knew art history, foreign languages and the history of the city"

I was a gondolier for 46 years and during that time I met many inspiring people, some of whom worked in cinema and theatre, such as Gary Cooper and Raymond Burr. Venice was a meeting point, a place where foreigners and tourists came and stayed for extended periods. Everyone was curious to discover not only the city but also its history.

Venice has long been home to some influential figures. Not the birthplace but a spiritual home, somewhere people choose to come back to. There's Aldo Manuzio, the first modern editor as we know it, and Vincenzo Maria Coronelli, famous for his globes and founding the Accademia degli Argonauti, the first association of geographers. More recently there has been American composer Cole Porter, who used to rent Ca' Rezzonico during the summer. A gondolier friend of my father's said that every night during Porter's stay the palazzo hosted the most fabulous parties.

Before he died, Porter wanted to come to Venice one last time; he stayed at the Palazzo Gritti and I saw him in Piazza San Marco in a wheelchair. He wasn't alone in wanting to return to Venice at the end of his life: Wagner died here too.

I've been fortunate to be able to meet a colourful cast of characters in my time;

some of them even specifically asked for me when they came to the city. But things are different now. The role of the gondolier has changed because life in Venice has changed. Tourists are in a hurry and rarely stay for more than a week. The gondolier used to be a sort of cicerone: he knew art history, foreign languages and the history of the city. He learned all of it at a specific school that implemented the knowledge that the older generation passed on to the next.

A gondola ride used to be a chance to learn new things about this mysterious city. Wagner drew inspiration from his gondolier, Luigi Trevisan, known as Ganasseta. Turning a corner in the moonlight, the gondolier shouted, "Oeh", the gondolier's cry. This is how the third act of *Tristan und Isolde* begins. Likewise, composers such as Franz Liszt and Gioacchino Rossini took inspiration from the gondola itself.

These are strange times for the city and its craftsmanship – we were 180,000, today we're 50,000 – and you can't live off memories. But I've travelled the world and I believe that Venice is still a magical city. To me, being a gondolier was never work; it was more of a pastime, a pleasure. And I would do it all over again. — (M)

Famous people buried in Venice

01 Ezra Pound
Expat US poet and writer who spent many years in Italy.
02 Igor Stravinsky
Russian composer, conductor and pianist.
03 Joseph Brodsky
Winner of the Nobel prize for literature.

ABOUT THE WRITER: Born in a family of gondoliers, Gino Macropodio steered visitors through Venice's canals for 46 years. He enjoyed the crowded years of cinema and is a keeper of the city's secrets.

Venice Essays

ESSAY 09

The biennale
A guide for the uninitiated

Alternating between art and architecture, the biennale showcases installations and entertainment alike. But with so much to see, where to start?

by Aaron Betsky, curator

Find yourself in Venice at a certain time of year and you will likely notice a higher concentration of visitors clad in head-to-toe black. You might spot them sashaying down streets, partying on yachts or snapping up the chicest hotel rooms and restaurant tables in town. You will also notice art in the most unexpected places. It must be biennale season.

Every summer the city's palazzos, courtyards, churches and disused warehouse spaces are appropriated by artists, architects and their enablers. The world's creatives come in their droves, lured by world-class installations and the promise of a good party. On odd years the Biennale Arte sets up camp; in the intervening years it's the turn of the somewhat smaller Biennale Architettura. Though the crowds can be unrelenting, both events offer untold opportunities to see great things – and glamorous people.

For the uninitiated, the trick is to wrangle an invitation to the vernissage – or pre-opening period – when the artists, designers, architects, curators and collectors fly in from around the globe to see the exhibitions before the hoi polloi. This is when the installations that involve some form of performance are at their best (and the parties their most bacchanalian). But if you miss the boat, fear not: the biennales run for a full six months after this.

The biennale makes use of spaces around the city that are normally off-limits or neglected. The first took place in the public gardens of the Giardini in 1895 and the event has been held there ever since. Off-season the park can feel a little forlorn, the various country pavilions out of use and shuttered up – though that does make it a quiet refuge from the city's throngs. During the biennale it becomes a space where art and architecture can bloom.

Since 1980 the biennale has adopted a second location: the Arsenale. Over the years the biennale organisation has been clawing the 46-hectare medieval armament and shipbuilding site away from the Italian navy, brick

Venice Essays

Biennale tips

01 How to arrive
Take a water taxi directly from the airport to your hotel.
02 When to visit
During its opening days, rubbing shoulders with artists, architects and collectors.
03 Other attractions
Carlo Scarpa's Fondazione Querini Stampalia.

hall by brick hall. The centrepiece of the complex is the *corderie*, a 330-metre-long stretch of 10-metre-tall spaces originally used by shipbuilders to make ropes. Like most curators, when I designed the 2008 Biennale Architettura I set out to shock and awe in this space.

The exhibits continue around the corner, turning from official displays to presentations by different countries. In recent years the biennale has also moved across the alley into a two-storey hall filled with more exhibitions – and further renovations are underway. I tend to bypass the Italian Pavilion (sadly it's often disappointing) and head to the Giardino delle Vergini (Garden of the Virgins) at Venice's edge. I had the pleasure of carving out its rear section into a series of outdoor rooms in 2008. The curved grass ramps that landscape architect Kathryn Gustafson installed that year are still in place; the perfect spot to recharge before continuing on your way.

A few years ago a back door was built in the garden wall. Now you can slip out without retracing what amounts to some 2km of steps, wind your way through the quiet working-class neighbourhood of Castello and, using the signs that the biennale has installed like breadcrumbs at crucial corners, find your way to the front door of the Giardini.

Here the main axis leads directly to the other space that the curator has at his or her disposal: the Central Pavilion, a maze of galleries in which it's easy to get lost. Once you've found the exit (almost inevitably through the gift shop) you're free to explore pavilions from two dozen countries that are strewn around the grounds, some dating back to the end of the 19th century and others modernist inventions (*see page 118*). Don't miss the back area across a canal, where countries such as Poland and Brazil often present surprising exhibitions.

Once you're done (it usually takes me about two days) and have taken a much-needed nap, the fun really begins. All over Venice, countries and groups that don't have a permanent pavilion or space rent out palazzos, warehouses,

"Every summer the city's palazzos, courtyards, churches and disused warehouse spaces are appropriated by artists, architects and their enablers"

shops or whatever they can find to display their art or architecture. Some of them are listed in the biennale's official guide (for a hefty fee) but the best are discovered by flyers or word of mouth.

The same is true for the parties, which seem to appear around corners where you least expect them; the official ones run out of prosecco and food almost immediately but the pop-ups and unofficial events can be lavish. My favourite is the Dark Side: a dinner and discussion held in secret locations during the opening days of the Biennale Architettura. It starts at about 22.00 and usually descends into the inarticulate, if passionate, stage of arguments at some point between 02.00 and 03.00.

As curator I had a *motoscafo* (speed boat) at my disposal during the opening days, so even the events on small outlying islands were easily accessible. Now I trudge around like everybody else, waiting for the waterbus, trying to figure out where everything is and discovering new facets of this labyrinthine city. The added bonus is that you always discover another hidden part of Venice along the way. — (M)

ABOUT THE WRITER: Aaron Betsky is the dean of the Frank Lloyd Wright School of Architecture. In 2008 he curated the 11th Biennale Architettura. Trained as an architect, he is a critic, author and curator.

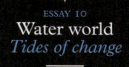

ESSAY 10
Water world
Tides of change

Water is the lifeblood of Venice and residents are long accustomed to adapting their lives according to its ebb and flow. But recent events suggest the city's relationship with its long-term protector may need to be reimagined.

by Chiara Rimella, Monocle

Raise your eyes skyward in Venice and you'll see lanky clock towers, lace-like window guards and domes plump as ice-cream scoops. Yet if you want to really understand this city and its architecture you have to look beyond what meets the eye – underwater in fact. Here millions of pilings are hammered into the slimy seabed, the wood petrified and hardened by layers of mud and a lack of oxygen. This thick, upside-down forest is the city's foundation, supporting its grand palazzos, cobbled alleyways, piazzas and many centuries of design history.

Water – the resistance against it and the coexistence with it – defines Venice. The decision to build such a place was bizarre but also justified: the location on stilts in the middle of a lagoon became not only an instrumental factor in its power and success but the very condition for it. Today the empire and fleet may be long gone but this improbable setting is still important: it's a living bricks-and-mortar testament to the fact that constructing a city in balance with nature is possible and to be recommended. Venice walks a tightrope of captivating vulnerability and equally mesmerising durability.

As well as bolstering trade in the early days, being surrounded by the billows has saved the city in more recent times too. Akin to protective walls, the waves have not only kept would-be attackers at bay but also prevented the city from expanding outwards. As a result, Venice has been spared from haphazardly built, sprawling suburbs. When more land was needed its outskirts were transplanted to the mainland, in Mestre, today connected by the long Ponte della Libertà.

Advocates of modernity at all costs have tried to label Venice as a prisoner of its lagoon. Yet concessions to industrialising the coast with the chemical plants of Porto Marghera stand in ghastly comparison with the farsighted approach of the Magistrato alle Acque (Venice Water Authority), first founded in 1501. For centuries its activities have subordinated commercial interests to the public good of the city and its watery landscape.

The key to life in Venice lies in thinking that water is not the enemy but a tricky, fickle friend. It's the attitude that guides responses to *acqua alta*: the

> **Fast facts on Mose, the new flood-defence system**
> ---
> **01 Protection**
> It will feature 57 flood barriers.
> **02 Deflection**
> It can see off tides that are up to three metres tall.
> **03 Installation**
> It's budgeted at a whopping €5.5bn.

periodical flooding of the city that takes place when a high tide coincides with low atmospheric pressure and a warm wind. Architectural measures to protect oneself (and one's belongings) from the rising waters do exist but they are pretty flimsy: symptoms of resignation perhaps, or rather an acceptance of the collateral of this age-old cohabitation. Upon the sounding of the haunting drawn-out sirens that signal that *acqua alta* is coming, stoical Venetians get up and place water-tight bulkheads on their door frames. Some bring their wellies to work if their route takes them beyond the boardwalks that spring up across the city's *campi*, or hitch a ride on the back of a tall friend.

It's rare for even substantial architectural solutions to strive to completely keep the water out: the usual approach is to let it in gently, control it, master it. Venice's pre-eminent architect Carlo Scarpa was famously inspired and enamoured by its ebb and flow. In 1961 he was commissioned to find a way to protect the Fondazione Querini Stampalia (*see page 107*) from the high tide. His response? "It's a matter of containing it, of using it like a luminous, reflective material." The famous staircase he built is all the more fascinating for being surrounded by the water flowing in.

This city was, after all, born with canals long before *calli* and its bridges were built well into its existence. The waterways were the main thoroughfares and palazzos

> "The key to life lies in thinking that water is not the enemy but a tricky, fickle friend. It's the attitude that guides responses to 'acqua alta': the periodical flooding of the city"

accordingly had their entrances on the canal-side: sailors don't get their feet wet when the tide rises. But *acqua alta* is turning into an issue for the city – or at least, the symptom of a problem. While tides as high as the terrible flood of 1966 are still relatively rare, the frequency of *acqua alta* has increased steadfastly. A century ago, San Marco used to be flooded five to seven times a year: by 2010 that number had jumped to 156. The opening of vast port mouths and enlargement of submarine passages to let big ships through (including those controversial cruiseships) are partly to blame, as is global warming.

Entrances to buildings may be raised and inhabitants can move out of ground floors but the issue will never be resolved by shooting up (designs such as JDS Architect's Aqualta 2060, a system of skyscrapers planted like a corolla around the city, can't help but have a distinctly dystopian flavour). Instead the answer is once again to be discovered underwater.

It is here, through safeguarding the hidden grooves of its seabed that help regulate the tides, that the city can find protection. Nature doesn't need Venice but Venice needs water. And if the city cares about maintaining its beautiful balance with the ecosystem that surrounds it, it had better continue to consider the water its most ancient – and valuable – of allies. — (M)

ABOUT THE WRITER: Chiara Rimella writes about design and architecture for MONOCLE and first fell for Venice when she visited the Biennale Architettura. Reporting for this guide, she made it through the trip without getting her feet wet (but a seagull did snatch a *cichèto* from her hand in Piazza San Marco).

ESSAY 11
Identity crisis
Masks in Venetian society

Allowing all citizens of Venice to mingle at Carnevale, no matter their social status, masks took on a great cultural significance in the Middle Ages – and they're still used today.

by Laura Morelli, art historian

Nobody knows exactly when, how or why Venetians began to wear masks in public. The earliest accounts are laws stating what citizens could not do while wearing them: a law of 1268 forbade masked people from playing certain games; another 13th-century order prohibited them from gambling; and in 1339 the republic outlawed vulgar disguises and visiting convents when masked. We can only assume that these laws were established because people had been pushing it.

From the Middle Ages, masks were associated with Carnevale, the annual festival in Catholic countries that traditionally takes place in the 10 days preceding

Venice
Essays

Lent. Lent being about abstinence, the days leading up to it were a chance to overindulge: in food, drink and merry-making. Venice held its first Carnevale in the 11th century and celebrations extended through the city's streets and squares, a free-for-all including parades, balls, street music, tomfoolery and general revelry.

Under the laws of the republic, Venetians were allowed to wear masks between St Stephen's Day on 26 December and the end of Carnevale on Shrove Tuesday (or Mardi Gras: Fat Tuesday), which usually falls in February. This official period of mask-wearing was the one time of year when social divisions were blurred. Members of any social class could play with a new identity behind the anonymity of a mask and a rented costume.

By the 17th century, however, Carnevale was not the only setting for the wearing of masks. The traditional *baùta* mask could be worn at significant political and law-making affairs, when it was important for Venetian citizens to remain anonymous in the interest of fair decision-making. In this turn of events, masks helped to sustain Venice's societal structure rather than flip it on its head.

Over the centuries a variety of mask styles were developed. The earliest Carnevale masks were simple – a plain white or black moulded form with cutouts for eyes – but more elaborate models were developed during the Renaissance. By the 18th century some of the most commonly worn mask types were based on characters from the Commedia dell'Arte, a popular theatre genre whose stock characters – heroes, clowns, patricians and servants – were instantly recognisable. Most of these character masks were half-masks, keeping the mouth free so that the actor could be heard.

Early Venetian mask-makers, or *mascareri*, belonged to the same trade guild as painters. Venetian guilds abided by strict written rules called *mariregole* that governed integral aspects of members' lives, from regulating their apprentices and salaries to dowering their daughters, ministering to their sick, providing for their retired and burying their dead. In short they were well looked after but it was expected that a mask-maker

> "Members of any social class could play with a new identity behind the anonymity of a mask"

Mask types

01 Baùta
A stark faceplate traditionally paired with a hooded cloak.
02 Volto
A "face in the crowd": a simple oval with cutouts.
03 Moretta
Women secured this mask by holding a button between their teeth.

would pass the torch to the next generation and preserve the craft.

Mostly it worked – Venetian masks are perhaps more popular than ever, no matter the time of year – and although some makers now use materials such as leather, glass and ceramic, there are still those who follow tradition by working primarily in papier mâché. During Carnevale, private balls such as the exclusive Ballo del Doge cater to dignitaries who want to recreate the magic, including mask-wearing. The tradition continues, in part, thanks to these internationally famed events.

But today's lively tourism trade is a double-edged sword: Carnevale masks flood into Venice each year, imported from overseas and passed off as authentic. Recently, legal regulations have tightened and art organisations have developed trademarks and new alliances to help protect their artistic heritage.

Many Venetian mask-makers welcome visitors into their studios to watch them work and buy off-the-shelf or custom designs. Take advantage of the chance to learn more about this art and meet the *mascarer* in person. It's also the best guarantee you pay the lowest possible price for a truly authentic and handmade work. — (M)

ABOUT THE WRITER: Laura Morelli is an art historian and novelist. Her shopping guides, *Made in Venice* and *Made in Italy*, encourage the discovery of artisanal traditions and her debut novel, *The Gondola Maker*, won an Ippy award for best historical fiction.

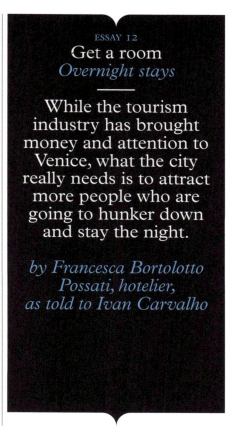

ESSAY 12
Get a room
Overnight stays

While the tourism industry has brought money and attention to Venice, what the city really needs is to attract more people who are going to hunker down and stay the night.

by Francesca Bortolotto Possati, hotelier, as told to Ivan Carvalho

My family has been in the hotel business in Venice for three generations. My grandfather, who was a shipbuilder from Liguria, purchased the Bauer property on the Canal Grande in 1930. He remodelled it and added a modernist 1940s façade that was very pronounced; a bit controversial in conservative Venice. I took over in the late 1990s and today we have several properties, with 300 staff and more than 300 guestrooms.

Managing a hotel here has unique challenges. You need to invest in waterproofing, which my grandfather did in the 1950s. I've overseen work to ensure that our interiors are protected from flooding up to two metres.

Venice
Essays

When you live in Venice you experience something of an island syndrome. The setting here is different and life on the mainland feels far away; you feel more Venetian than Italian. What's on everyone's mind today is the number of tourists invading the city. The boom began back in the 1980s when airlines made travel more accessible. Americans and others rediscovered the city and fell in love with its beauty. They brought welcome attention to Venice but now the city receives too much love; it has become a burden.

> "Daytrippers come like waves every day but they don't try to understand the destination in which they find themselves; it's a hit-and-run experience"

As a hotelier I want visitors, not tourists. Visitors invest time in a city. Today we see so many daytrippers; during Carnevale upwards of 130,000 a day. Of the 23 million who visit each year, only six million stay a night. They come like waves every day but they don't try to understand the destination in which they find themselves; it's a hit-and-run experience.

Even when the city hosts the biennale, which runs for six months, most of the visitors and hotel stays are concentrated in the first two weeks. We used to welcome a more select group from all over the world: the Grand Tour. They invested time in the city. In the 1950s we even had a daily seaplane service between Venice and Trieste but that stopped because locals were worried about a plane landing so close to their historical city. Today the concern has turned to big cruise ships, which don't bring in that many passengers – fewer than two million – compared to the total number of visitors but whose presence in the canals can damage the city's foundations.

One way to attract longer stays is by investing in contemporary culture. Venice

Tips for longer stays

01 **If you want peace and quiet**
Visit in low season: November, December and January.

02 **If it's art you're after**
Brave the busy first weeks of the biennale.

03 **Where to find lodging**
On Giudecca, the coolest spot in the city.

is a spa for the mind; it's the perfect place to discover new things and expand your knowledge. We, The Bauer Hotel Group, have partnered with the Università Ca' Foscari to put on an annual literature festival called Incroci di Civiltà, welcoming leading writers from around the world. We've created a literary award that we present for this occasion. Since 2011 I've also sponsored a cultural non-profit called Zucca Project Space (*see page 90*), which promotes contemporary art, architecture and film and oversees venues on Giudecca and in San Marco.

In the future we need to give residents a bigger voice so that they can take ownership of their city. We may number only 50,000 but we value and cherish Venice; it's our jewel. We need to encourage more young couples to live here. We need more services – from pharmacies to schools – not just shops for tourists. After all, who are better ambassadors for a city than its citizens? — (M)

ABOUT THE WRITER: Venetian native Francesca Bortolotto Possati is president and CEO of The Bauer Hotel Group. She also serves on the board of directors of the Save Venice organisation.

Venice
Culture

Culture
—— Painting the town

Museums and galleries
Well hung

Venice's culture scene is nothing if not varied: classical churches contain masterpieces by Venetian greats such as Titian, Tintoretto and Veronese; palazzos are piled high with works by both local and international artists; and commercial galleries can be found down even the narrowest of *calli*. You might assume that modern art is hard to come by but head to the likes of the Collezione Peggy Guggenheim and you'll find yourself surrounded by 20th and 21st-century marvels.

Operas and concerts take place not only in sumptuous theatres but also in crumbling churches and palazzos, making performances more intimate. Similarly, a handful of libraries are as much museums as quiet refuges in which to read.

Venice falls short when it comes to cinemas, a surprise for the host of a world-famous film festival; likewise the party scene is a little more subdued than in Casanova's day. That is until biennale, when the whole city becomes one big whirlwind of activity.

①
Palazzo Fortuny, San Marco
Aged beauty

This four-storey gothic palazzo is only open during temporary exhibitions and, when it is, it should not be missed. It's the former home and atelier of Mariano Fortuny, who retired here in the late 1930s, and the museum pays tribute to his eclectic career with sections dedicated to themes that vary from set design to textiles.

Alongside exposed brickwork, Fortuny fabrics make for luxurious backdrops, while the Spanish designer's signature lamps cast the rooms in a splendid light. Off the overflowing first-floor salone is a room adorned with a mural that he painted; look up and you'll see monkeys scrambling over the arches. On the less-crowded second floor is another treat: Fortuny's private library, beautifully intact like the sketchbook of pressed flowers within.
3780 Campo San Beneto, 30126
+39 041 520 0995
fortuny.visitmuve.it

Venice Culture

Venice's masters

You don't have to go to a museum to see a masterpiece in Venice: at your fingertips are countless churches and confraternities full of monumental paintings. In the 16th century, Venice was the artistic playground of three fiercely talented and competitive painters: Tiziano Vecellio (Titian), Jacopo Comin (Tintoretto) and Paolo Caliari (Veronese). Here are three places to find some of their best devotional works, as well as the artists themselves: each is buried in the same church as his art.

01 Chiesa della Madonna dell'Orto, Cannaregio: The parish church of Tintoretto is home to more than 10 of his paintings. The biggest and best are the jam-packed canvases that flank the altar: "The Adoration of the Golden Calf" and "The Last Judgment" (both painted in the mid-1500s).
madonnadellorto.org

02 Basilica di Santa Maria Gloriosa dei Frari, San Polo: As soon as you enter this enormous Franciscan church, more commonly known as I Frari, you'll see Titian's golden masterpiece: his "Assumption of the Virgin" (1518) hangs above the high altar.
basilicadeifrari.it

03 Chiesa di San Sebastiano, Dorsoduro: Over the course of his life, Veronese adorned this church from top to toe. To see how his style progressed over the years, start with the Old Testament paintings in the sacristy and end with the altarpiece of the Virgin Mary.
chorusvenezia.org

Keeping watch — Fritz Koenig's "Chariot" (1957) overlooks the garden

Conversation starter

Founded in 2011 by Alessandro Possati, Zuecca Project Space is a non-profit cultural organisation that works with different art forms, institutions and artists to promote a creative exchange of ideas.
zueccaprojects.com

Venice Culture

 Collezione Peggy Guggenheim, Dorsoduro
Lady of the house

Peggy Guggenheim was an American heiress and impresario of the avant garde. Having amassed her collection in London, Paris and New York, she exhibited it at the biennale in 1948 and bought the single-storey Palazzo Venier dei Leoni on the Canal Grande the following year. Today the 18th-century palazzo hosts a permanent collection, an outdoor sculpture garden and temporary exhibitions of modern and contemporary art.

Peggy is ever present: Jackson Pollock, among her favourites, has his own room; Alexander Calder's "Silver Bedhead" (1946) was made for her; and her ashes are scattered in the garden. Then there's Marino Marini's "The Angel of the City" (1948), a sculpture that nods to her appetite for sex as well as art.
704 Fondamenta Venier dei Leoni, 30123
+39 041 240 5411
guggenheim-venice.it

③ Gallerie dell'Accademia, Dorsoduro
Pick and choose

This historic museum is located in the Scuola Grande of Santa Maria della Carità, one of Venice's oldest lay fraternities. Its rich collection was made possible by Napoleon in a roundabout way: he confiscated swathes of art from churches, guilds and convents and deposited them here in 1807.

It's best to cherry-pick your way through the museum. The first gallery is overlooked by gilded cherubim; room 20 is devoted to Bellini and Carpaccio; and room 24 is all about Titian's "Presentation of the Virgin" (1534-38).

1050 Campo della Carità, 30123
+39 041 520 0345
gallerieaccademia.org

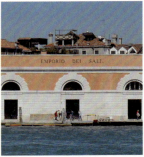

About time — The galleries trace the history of art in Venice

④ Fondazione Emilio e Annabianca Vedova, Dorsoduro
Art in motion

Avant garde artist Emilio Vedova's vast body of work was organised by his wife Annabianca, with whom he lived on the Zattere for 50 years. Today, in two spaces that are open from May to November, the foundation arranges exhibitions to highlight its importance in terms of the history of 20th-century art.

The exhibitions themselves are dynamic – many see Vedova's art in dialogue with that of a contemporary artist, from Calder to Kiefer – but their display in the Magazzino del Sale, one of nine salt warehouses on the waterfront, goes one step further. After Vedova's death in 2006, Renzo Piano restored the space and created a hi-tech machine that stores and suspends the works in an ever-changing sequence – a rare glimpse of a "curator" at work.

50 Zattere, 30123
+39 041 241 0833
fondazionevedova.org

Venice
Culture

⑤ Ca' Pesaro, San Polo
Old and new

This 17th-century palazzo on the Canal Grande is home to two institutions. The Galleria Internazionale d'Arte Moderna is a worthy introduction to 19th and 20th-century art, with a permanent collection of paintings and sculptures by the likes of Kandinsky and Moore. The tiny Museo d'Arte Orientale, at the top of a creaky staircase, could be a nice change if you're into Japanese arms and armour.

Baldassare Longhena designed the palazzo and Gian Antonio Gaspari finished the building work in 1710. After the last Pesaro died it was eventually bought by the Bevilacqua family and bequeathed to the city as a modern-art museum in 1898. Although the Pesaros' great collection is gone, original frescoes and reliefs remain.
2076 Fondamenta de Ca' Pesaro, 30135
+39 041 721 127
capesaro.visitmuve.it

⑥ Tre Oci, Giudecca
In focus

Named after its three "eyes" – the arched windows that watch over San Marco from its façade – Tre Oci on Giudecca is a prime example of Venetian neo-gothic architecture. It was designed by painter Mario de Maria in 1913, acquired by the Fondazione di Venezia in 2000 and opened as an exhibition venue 12 years later.

Today it hosts workshops, screenings and art exhibitions, as well as the foundation's photographic collections, which include more than 100,000 images taken by the De Maria family.
43 Fondamenta delle Zitelle, 30133
+39 041 241 2332
treoci.org

> **Reliquary of the republic**
>
> Napoleon's former pad in Piazza San Marco is today home to the Museo Correr, the city's civic museum. Highlights include a collection of marble sculptures by Antonio Canova and the sumptuous chandelier-clad ballroom.
> *correr.visitmuve.it*

Venice Culture

⑦ Ca' Rezzonico, Dorsoduro
Pay and display

Ca' Rezzonico is a museum of 18th-century Venice – and an ode to the elite. Designed by Baldassare Longhena for the Bon family in 1649, the palazzo was bought by the Rezzonico family (Lombard bankers who paid to be members of Venice's nobility) in 1751 and the building work was completed by Giorgio Massari in 1756.

Architectural and painterly acts of social-climbing are everywhere: Massari created a regal air in the ballroom by doubling the height of the ceiling, while Giambattista Tiepolo promoted the Rezzonicos in the throne room with a fresco of Merit ascending to the Temple of Glory with the Libro d'Oro, a directory of nobles' names. The Longhi room is different: the genre pictures by Pietro Longhi openly poke fun at the social antics of the rich and famous.
314 Fondamenta Rezzonico, 30123
+39 041 241 0100
carezzonico.visitmuve.it

> **Front runner**
>
> Largely dedicated to research exhibitions, the Fondazione Prada is at the cutting edge of art exhibiting and discourse. Frequent events draw the most important contemporary artists and thinkers to Venice – and they rarely disappoint.
> *fondazioneprada.org*

⑧ Punta della Dogana, Dorsoduro
Dare to be different

Punta della Dogana, housed in what was once the republic's central customs house, is a modern-art museum that commands views across the Bacino di San Marco. Restored by Japanese architect Tadao Ando in 2009, it's now one of the few truly contemporary buildings in this ancient city – although it's impossible to tell from the outside. Inside, a sequence of large exhibition spaces of exposed brick and original wooden roof trusses are punctuated by spatial interventions cast in concrete. Unlike most Venetian museums, this one is dedicated to the new, the bold and the controversial.

Without a permanent collection, the museum pays tribute to the temporary; the private collection of its owner, François Pinault, is housed in its sister gallery in the Palazzo Grassi (*see page 96*) along the Canal Grande. Punta della Dogana is world renowned for its performance art, installations and large-scale works; there is also an excellent art-themed bookshop and a small café. Both are hidden gems and rarely overcrowded.
2 Fondamenta Salute, 30123
+39 041 240 1308
palazzograssi.it

> **Out of water**
>
> An ancient gondola greets visitors to Ca' Rezzonico

Venice
Culture

⑨ Arzanà, Cannaregio
Whatever floats your boat

Housed in a 15th-century *squero* (boat-building yard) that was churning out gondolas for Venice's high and mighty until the 1920s, this tiny two-room museum is packed to the sail-draped rafters with all manner of gondola and boat-building paraphernalia.

Rows of tools, swathes of rope and stacks of timber (a classic gondola is made from eight types of wood) compete for shelf space with model ships, fishing nets, duck-hunting decoys and lanterns. As well as telling the story of the boat-building craft in the lagoon, salvage and preservation are the primary concern. And while there is a fair amount of dust this is no musty mausoleum: the smell of wood polish hangs heavy on the air. Visits are by appointment only and hosted by a team of knowledgeable volunteers who can speak English or Italian.

1936D Calle Pignatte, 30121
arzana.org

095

Venice Culture

⑩
Palazzo Grassi, San Marco
Private eye

One of the most important 18th-century palazzos, this was in fact the last palace to be built on the Canal Grande before the fall of the Venetian republic in 1797. In 2005, 165 years after the Grassi family let it go, art collector François Pinault purchased the palazzo to house his private collection of modern and contemporary art. Renovated by Japanese architect Tadao Ando – who later also worked on its sister-gallery, Punta della Dogana (*see page 94*) – it reopened in 2006.

Crisp white exhibition spaces contrast with expertly preserved ornamental fresco work and decoration. Alongside contemporary art you'll find a stairwell frescoed by Michelangelo Morlaiter and Francesco Zanchi, as well as ceilings by Giambattista Canal and Christian Griepenkerl.
3225 Calle delle Carrozze, 30124
+39 041 240 1308
palazzograssi.it

⑪
Espace Louis Vuitton Venezia, San Marco
Talking shop

Who knew that above the Maison Louis Vuitton you would find a space devoted to both historical and contemporary art? Launched in 2013 by the Fondation Louis Vuitton, which has six exhibition venues around the world, Espace Louis Vuitton Venezia creates a dialogue between international contemporary art and the cultural heritage of Venice. In collaboration with the Fondazione Musei Civici di Venezia, it also funds the restoration of historical works.

Each exhibition sees an artist respond to a piece of Venetian history. In 2016 the foundation restored 18th-century models of museums and villas and paired them with designs for Frank Gehry's Fondation Louis Vuitton building in Paris and an in-situ creation by Daniel Buren.
1353 Calle del Ridotto, 30124
+39 041 884 4318
louisvuitton.com

Room with a view — A trompe-l'oeil loggia overlooks the staircase

Venice
Culture

Commercial galleries
Creative businesses

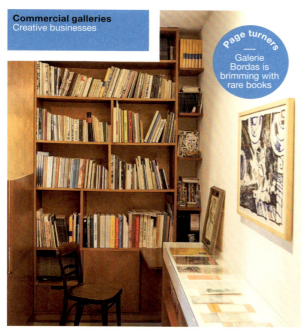

Page turners — Galerie Bordas is brimming with rare books

① Galerie Bordas, San Marco
Prints charming

This slip of a gallery in the city centre may be small but it has a big offering. Hervé Bordas, the nephew of the great printer and lithographer Fernand Mourlot, moved from Paris to Venice at the end of the 1980s to open a space dedicated to graphic art.

Original prints by modern and contemporary artists hang on the walls, while illustrated books, exhibition catalogues and other 20th-century art-historical documents line the wooden shelves. Organised by assistant curator Domenico Brancale (*pictured*), the gallery hosts one exhibition a year and, of course, publishes its own catalogues to accompany them. Over the past 25 years it has exhibited etchings and lithographs by internationally renowned artists such as Picasso, Miró, Braque and Barceló.
1994B Calle Drio la Chiesa, 30124
+ 39 041 522 4812
galerie-bordas.com

La Biennale

Each year, from May until November, Venice shines the spotlight on the contemporary: the Biennale Arte takes place in odd years, the Biennale Architettura in even. Founded in 1895, the biennale is now one of the most famous and influential cultural organisations in the world – and it also brings out the best of the city's museums and galleries.

While the action unfolds in the historic pavilions of the Giardini and the restored warehouses of the Arsenale, an array of collateral events and exhibitions encourage visitors to explore other parts of the city. Performances include music, cinema, theatre and dance but art and architecture are the main attractions. Both involve individual exhibitions by national pavilions and the International Exhibition by that year's chosen curator.

As well as discovering and promoting new trends on the art and architecture scenes, the biennale is a promotional tool for Venice and its cultural offering. It's also gaining a sharper social and political edge: amid 2016's refugee crisis, Chilean architect Alejandro Aravena's *Reporting from the Front* was a socially conscious Biennale Architettura.
labiennale.org

This is my gift to the art world...

Venice Culture

③ A plus A Gallery, San Marco
Into the mix

The official venue for the Slovenian Pavilion from 1998 to 2014, under the direction of curator Aurora Fonda, A plus A Gallery has long been a meeting point for Slovenian, Italian and international artists. Since 2015, Fonda and her partner-cum-gallery manager Sandro Pignotti have transformed the space into a private enterprise dedicated to contemporary art.

"It's a gallery for young artists," says Pignotti who, like his wife, moved to Venice to do a PhD. As well as exhibitions, which are accompanied by colourful catalogues produced with design studio M-L-XL (previously Tank Boys), the gallery has hosted The School for Curatorial Studies Venice since 2004. A platform for young artists, the offshoot invites students to learn about curating and contemporary art.
3073 Calle Malipiero, 30124
+39 041 277 0466
aplusa.it

② Marignana Arte, Dorsoduro
Family affair

A stone's throw from Punta della Dogana and the Collezione Peggy Guggenheim, Marignana Arte is at the centre of a contemporary-art hub. It was opened in 2013 by mother and daughter Emanuela Fadalti and Matilde Cadenti, both architects with a passion for art.

The duo restored the entire 15th-century palazzo, selling the apartments upstairs and establishing a gallery below. They work closely with a different international curator on each exhibition and host artists of varying degrees of experience.
141 Rio Terà dei Catecumeni, 30123
+39 041 522 7360
marignanaarte.it

Luckily gondolas move slowly

④ Massimo Micheluzzi, Dorsoduro
Glass act

Massimo Micheluzzi's gallery is an ode to its surroundings: monochrome pots recall marble palazzos and gradually undulating vases in various shades of blue allude to the lagoon.

The Venetian native (*pictured*) combines traditional glass-making techniques with a modernist sensibility. He designs and cold-carves the glass in his studio and oversees the blowing and hot-shaping in a Murano glassworks. He's exhibited all over the world and has permanent collections in the likes of The Metropolitan Museum of Art in New York.
1071 Ponte delle Maravegie, 30123
+39 041 528 2190

Venice
—— Culture

⑤ Alma Zevi, San Marco
Taking up residence

Curator and art historian Alma Zevi opened her eponymous gallery on a quiet square in San Marco in 2016. The single-storey space, located near Palazzo Grassi, hosts four contemporary-art exhibitions a year: a mix of group and solo shows of both emerging and established international artists who work in a variety of media.

While some exhibitions are organised conventionally – shipping in artworks from around the world – others are the result of residency programmes. Individual artists are invited to use the gallery as a temporary studio space and produce site-specific pieces that respond to the unique setting of Venice. Zevi also runs a residency programme in Celerina, Switzerland, which results in an annual summer exhibition.
3357 Salizzada San Samuele, 30124
+ 39 041 520 9197
almazevi.com

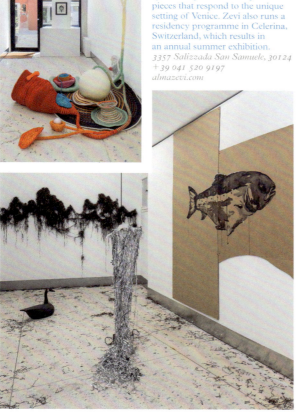

⑥ Giorgio Mastinu Fine Art, San Marco
Small wonder

"Documents that tell a story about the life and work of artists": that's how the bespectacled Giorgio Mastinu (*pictured*), who moved to Venice some 30 years ago to study architecture, describes the ephemera in his tiny gallery near Campo Santo Stefano. These documents include artists' books, invitations, photographs, prints and drawings – and the pocket-sized space in which they're displayed means the viewer can explore them up close.

Aside from the two windows – which Mastinu calls his "exhibition space" – the gallery is more of an archive; a space for research rather than displays. His main focus is Italian art and architecture after the Second World War but he also collaborates with contemporary international artists and museums.
2989 Calle dei Orbi, 30124
+ 39 347 182 8553
giorgiomastinufineart.it

Libraries and workshops
Between the lines

①
Biblioteca della Biennale, Castello
Stories of art

Housed within a restored wing of the Central Pavilion in the Giardini, the biennale library invites the public to explore international art and architecture year round. In fact the pavilion itself is worthy of exploration: not far from the reading rooms, connected by snappy red railings and staircases, is an inner garden designed by Carlo Scarpa.

On the shelves are more than 145,000 volumes on the history of art and architecture from the end of the 19th century onwards – and in a bid to break it down, books are alphabetised and grouped according to whether they have more or less than 100 pages. As well as catalogues from the biennale there are more than 3,000 periodicals on cultural pursuits such as music, theatre and dance.
859 Calle Paludo Sant'Antonio, 30122
+39 041 521 8939
labiennale.org

②
Bottega del Tintoretto, Cannaregio
Fine prints

In the 1500s Tintoretto used to live in the building next to this atelier. Today his influence lingers (together with a pungent smell of turpentine) in this dimly lit printing studio named in his honour.

A group of artists opened this laboratory in 1986 and kitted it out with antique presses and machines with which they still print work on commission. What attracts most visitors to the bottega are the courses held weekly between October and May, which range from lithography and etching to bookbinding and watercolour.
3400 Fondamenta dei Mori, 30121
+39 041 722 081
tintorettovenezia.it

Venice Culture

Live venues
Music and more

❶
Teatrino di Palazzo Grassi, San Marco
Third time's a charm

After renovating both the Palazzo Grassi and Punta della Dogana, François Pinault turned his attention to this *teatrino* (see page 104). The little theatre opened in 2013 and today holds events that often complement the displays in the two exhibition venues.

In its two foyers and 225-seat auditorium the minimalist theatre hosts more than 100 events a year, from artists' talks to conferences, screenings and concerts. The space is an ideal blank canvas for a film projection.
3225 Calle delle Carrozze, 30124
+39 041 523 1680
palazzograssi.it

❸
Biblioteche della Fondazione Giorgio Cini, Isola di San Giorgio Maggiore
Treasure island

The Fondazione Giorgio Cini, established by Count Vittorio Cini in 1951, is based in the former Benedictine monastery of San Giorgio Maggiore. The complex was designed in the early 1500s and today hosts the cultural institution, complete with two main libraries that cover – among other things – the history of art and Venice.

In 2009, Milanese architect Michele De Lucchi converted the monks' dormitory into the Nuova Manica Lunga; the tunnel-like space stretches along the upper wing, the cells now offices or rooms for special collections. A corridor of periodicals connects it to the ancient Longhena Library, which was designed by Baldassare Longhena and still features Franz Pauc's original wooden bookcases.
Isola di San Giorgio Maggiore, 30100
+39 041 271 0255
cini.it/biblioteche

❷
Teatro La Fenice, San Marco
Fiery performances

Venice's favourite theatre was founded in 1792 on the site of the Teatro San Benedetto, which burned down in 1774. Another fire destroyed the new theatre in 1836 and after it was rebuilt, there was a third blaze in 1996. In 2003 it reopened, complete with the original foyer and burn marks on its floor.

The theatre stages more than 100 operas a year, as well as ballets, symphonies and a contemporary repertoire. And the building itself is a spectacle: blue details echo the city's canals and the royal box is topped with the winged lion of Saint Mark.
1965 Campo San Fantin, 30124
+39 041 786 511
teatrolafenice.it

Making music

The Venice Music Project, now based in Saint George's Anglican Church in Campo San Vio, raises funds to restore art and architecture around the city by performing baroque compositions by Handel, Vivaldi and more.
venicemusicproject.it

Venice Culture

Musica a Palazzo, San Marco
Working the room

Opera can be intimidating but this cultural association, founded in 2005, breaks down the barriers between singers, instrumentalists and audience. It follows the 19th-century tradition of the chamber opera, which sees an opera performed by a small ensemble. The audience is also small and the stage in-the-round, allowing you to experience the action up close.

The backdrop is the 15th-century Palazzo Barbarigo Minotto overlooking the Canal Grande, among original baroque furnishings, stuccos and frescoes. Try to arrive early to bag the best seats but don't worry if you don't: every other act takes place in a different room. And there's no need to pre-order a drink because your ticket includes a glass (or two) of prosecco during the interval.
Fondamenta Duodo o Barbarigo, 30124
+39 340 971 7272
musicapalazzo.com

Teatro Malibran, Cannaregio
Second in command

Originally called the Teatro di San Giovanni Grisostomo, this 900-seat opera house was founded by the Grimani family in 1678. In 1835 it was renamed Teatro Malibran, after the singer Marcia Garcia Malibran performed on its stage, and in the 1960s it became a cinema. It showed films until the second fire struck La Fenice, when it was reverted to a theatre – pink-velvet curtain included – to restore Venice's cultural prestige.

The Malibran is run by the Fondazione Teatro La Fenice but, a typical Venetian theatre, it differs from its showstopping big sister. Although they share a classical-music, ballet and opera season, the Malibran draws a younger crowd with jazz and contemporary ballet. It also hosts smaller operas: the likes of *La Bohème* are reserved for La Fenice.
5873 Campiello Malibran, 30131
+39 041 965 1975
teatrolafenice.it

Teatro alle Tese, Castello
Setting sail

At the heart of the Arsenale, the former shipbuilding site of the Venetian navy, are the Tese Cinquecentesche: warehouses where sails were stretched in the 16th century. Attributed to the Italian architect Jacopo Sansovino, these four brick buildings connected by vast arches now host the Teatro alle Tese.

This 400-seat theatre was established in 2000 and syncs with the biennale: it's only open in spring and summer to time with the exhibitions (and because there's no heating). Unlike the nearby Teatro Piccolo Arsenale, which was conceived as a cinema and theatre from the beginning, this is a non-traditional space that has flexible seating and a mobile stage. It hosts major acts in music, theatre and dance.
2169 Campo della Tana, 30124
+39 041 521 8818
labiennale.org

All that jazz

A night on the tiles is a rare thing in Venice but the live music at the Venice Jazz Club in Dorsoduro is sure to get you moving. As well as the VJC Quartet, the intimate space hosts Italian and international groups.
venicejazzclub.com

Venice — Culture

Reel deal

Venice has fewer cinemas than you'd expect. During festival season, many screenings take place at the Palazzo del Cinema on Lido. But locals in search of a cosier option prefer the Giorgione off Rio Terà dei Franceschi or the Cinema Rossini at Salita del Teatro.

Media round-up
Word on the street

Venice on film

01 **Top Hat, 1935:** Three years after the city's inaugural international film festival, the silky canals were cast as a backdrop for Fred Astaire and Ginger Rogers to dance under the Venetian sunset in the finale of this great American musical.

02 **Senso, 1954:** Luchino Visconti's story of a doomed love affair between a troubled countess and an Austrian lieutenant is swept up in an operatic vision of the city.

03 **Death in Venice, 1971:** Perhaps the most famous film to feature the city, Visconti's classic adaptation of the Thomas Mann novel won a ceremonial prize at Cannes.

04 **Don't Look Now, 1973:** Nicolas Roeg's dark vision of Venice was based on a short story by Daphne du Maurier and stars Donald Sutherland and Julie Christie as a couple tormented by a clairvoyant.

05 **The Talented Mr Ripley, 1999:** In Patricia Highsmith's 1955 novel – as well as this screen adaptation – Venice offers a brief moment of calm during a cat-and-mouse game of trickery.

① Media
Reading material

Venetian publications are few and far between but these will give you a good introduction to the city.

Free bimonthly magazine ❶ *Cultura Venezia* is a point of reference for both residents and tourists, listing upcoming cultural events. ❷ *Inventario* is just that: an inventory of art, architecture and design, published three times a year. ❸ *Officina* is the free bimonthly magazine of Officina, a cultural and educational association founded by three graduates of the Università Iuav di Venezia in 2014. It covers architecture, design and technology.

Regional daily ❹ *La Nuova di Venezia e Mestre* is a popular choice when it comes to national, international and local news. ❺ *Il Gazzettino*, one of Italy's most successful regional daily newspapers, is the other option; its front pages are splashed with national and international news, while local affairs are found within.

② Radio Ca' Foscari
Listen in

Launched in 2007, Radio Ca' Foscari is an online station managed by students and staff at the eponymous university located in the lagoon city. Staff put on a range of programmes that cover topics such as food, film, sport and literature.

The weekly line-up offers regular shows as well as limited-run offerings; in the past, the latter has included a cultural series that saw the director of the Collezione Peggy Guggenheim delve into the history behind some of the museum's most prized artworks. A food show creatively presents recipes to listeners: for example, to the music of Vivaldi, the host gives a rundown on the best ways to make fish soup and offers a backstory on various foods. Another show, *Tea and a Book*, proposes a novel to curl up with each week and suggests which type of tea would best accompany it.
radiocafoscari.it

⑦ Ⓓ Venice
Design and architecture

Design and architecture
—— Building excitement

Venice intrigues and beguiles in equal measure. Its improbable, otherworldly splendour comes from buildings that appear to float on the lagoon, giving the city a dreamlike quality.

Once a great trading hub, Venice built up its wealth for all the world to see; the Canal Grande's palazzos and the innumerable churches are testament to that. Architects have used the city not so much as a template but as a temple and sometimes, hidden in among the historic grandeur, there are some surprising modernist twists; Venetian Carlo Scarpa's delicate interventions make him a 20th-century great.

Occasionally foreigners have been allowed to build here but as the city's newest bridge testifies, additions tend to be contentious. Even so, the Biennale Architettura and the design of other (sometimes unrealised) modern and contemporary projects show that Venice is more than a floating museum: it's a gently evolving masterpiece.

Contemporary
Recent additions

①
Ponte della Costituzione, Santa Croce/Cannaregio
Troubled bridge over water

This elegant crossing – often referred to as the Ponte di Calatrava, after its architect Santiago Calatrava – bears many of its Spanish creator's signature features, notably a skeletal structure that supports the walkway above.

Unfortunately Venice's new bridge has been beset with problems since opening in 2008: wheelchair access was overlooked in the design and the awkward gradient of the steps has led to injuries. But there's no denying its necessity (it connects two of Venice's transport hubs) and graceful presence.
Ponte della Costituzione, 30100

②
Teatrino di Palazzo Grassi, San Marco
Small wonder

This *teatrino* (little theatre) was designed by Japanese architect Tadao Ando and is used for everything from talks to concerts (*see page 101*). Theatre-goers enter via a tiny alley behind the Palazzo Grassi and are transported into the futuristic world of Ando's aesthetic.

The rectangular auditorium is encased within an irregular, lozenge-shaped floorplan. Other spaces are further accentuated by the use of shiny Marmorino stucco, the only typically Venetian detail of Ando's building.
3225 Calle delle Carrozze, 30124
+39 041 523 1680
palazzograssi.it

Venice
Design and architecture

④
Law Courts, Santa Croce
Legal assembly

There's something surreal about Piazzale Roma, where motorised traffic hits Venice and can go no further. The latest addition is the Law Courts, completed by Treviso-based C+S Associati in 2012.

The building is topped with a pitched roof and is sandwiched between the much lower pitched roofs of the former tobacco works to the south and the larger (flat-roofed) carpark to the north. The dark tone of the pre-oxidised copper cladding gives the building a slightly ominous presence but the overall impact is not unwelcome in this peculiar corner of Venice.
430 Cittadella della Giustizia, 30135

③
Former Junghans area, Giudecca
Time for a change

This residential district on Giudecca's south side was born of a competition in 1995, won by the office of Milanese architect Cino Zucchi. It repurposes land occupied by an old Junghans watch and clock factory, abandoned since the 1970s.

The neighbourhood, which was completed in 2002, feels distinctly modern and varied now, retaining aspects of the industrial fabric such as the large brick chimney. The A2 and A3 blocks are mixed-use and with the restaurant, bar and large *campo* in front, make for a convincingly Venetian urban composition.
Campo Junghans, 30133

105

Venice
Design and architecture

Carlo Scarpa
Shape shifter

Daring design — The striking overhanging roof is a bold move

⑤
Cimitero di San Michele, San Michele
Death in Venice

Since the 19th century the Isola di San Michele has been home to Venetians who have left the land of the living. As in life, however, space is a rather rare commodity in Venice so in 1998 the city decided that it would expand this square island cemetery by reclaiming land from the lagoon.
 British architect David Chipperfield won the competition to design the new burial grounds and the first of his complex of tightly packed rectangular courtyards was completed in 2007. Sombre monumentality is something that he specialises in and in this setting it has been used to great effect. Stacking graves in box-like structures is common in Italy but with his intimate and peaceful courtyards Chipperfield has managed to add beauty to a sad situation.
Isola di San Michele, 30135

①
Università Iuav di Venezia entrance, Santa Croce
Making an entrance

This entrance to the Università Iuav di Venezia is unusually assertive for Carlo Scarpa. This may be because, completed in 1985, it was realised some six years after the Venetian master's death by his co-worker Sergio Los.
 It's a less delicate style (see, for example, the roof that seems to float above the passageway) but it's nonetheless full of Scarpa's signature quirks. Look out for the postmodernist arrangement of the old neoclassical doorway, which has been surrounded by a pool.
191 Santa Croce, 30135
+39 041 257 1726
iuav.it

In good shape

No other Venetian has shaped all that is modern in the city like Scarpa – quite an achievement considering he never studied architecture. Born in 1906, his passion lay in Venice's rich visual history, as well as that of Japan. He also loved and designed glassware throughout his career.

Venice
Design and architecture

② Fondazione Querini Stampalia, Castello
Foundations of innovation

In 1868 Giovanni Querini Stampalia donated this palazzo to the foundation that bears his name but it was not until 1949 that it was decided to restore much of the building and make proper use of it. Scarpa was engaged to renovate and transform the ground level and the courtyard at the back.

The building itself was extremely prone to flooding and had been severely damaged by water entry; Scarpa's solution was to build a raised stone gangway that regulates the water. Together with beautifully sculpted steps leading to the water gates and the wonderful garden created from the courtyard, it lends an abundance of architectural intrigue to the building.
5252 Santa Maria Formosa, 30122
+39 041 271 1411
querinistampalia.org

Venice
Design and architecture

Bright idea
Light enters via second-floor wooden grids

Venice — Design and architecture

③ Negozio Olivetti, San Marco
Type setting

Scarpa was commissioned by Adriano Olivetti in 1958 to create the Negozio Olivetti. Although *negozio* (shop) indicates that the space might merely be a showroom for Olivetti's typewriters and counting machines, the purpose was a cultural investment in the brand. In Olivetti's words, it was to be a "business card" for the company.

Scarpa got to work with the precision and attention to detail with which he became synonymous. A linear plan developed, transcending the space by creating an architectural promenade with the use of African teak on the balconies and bridge, as well as slabs of the finest marble. Scarpa's staircase is a masterpiece, its irregular form both perplexing and harmonious; something repeated all over the Negozio Olivetti, a true gem of Venetian modern.
101 Piazza San Marco, 30124
+39 041 522 8387
negozioolivetti.it

④ Aula Mario Baratto, Dorsoduro
Modernist flourishes

Ca' Foscari is one of the city's most important palazzos, dating from the 15th century, and Scarpa worked on it at various stages between the 1930s and 1950s. He started in 1935 with the *aula magna* (great hall) of the university that has been housed here since the 19th century. The magnificent space – now called the Aula Mario Baratto – is dominated by high Venetian gothic windows and filled with Scarpa's masterful adaptations.

Rather than recreating original features, Scarpa carefully added modernist layers, notably a screen of wood-framed windows. Instead of mimicking or obscuring the iconic Poliforma shapes (pointed arches with crosses for windows) they provide a new interpretation. As do the crafted wooden screens added to transform the space into a modern lecture theatre in 1956.
3246 Ca' Foscari, 30123
+39 041 234 8111
unive.it

And that's bridge photo number 1,001 of the day

7 D Venice
Design and architecture ———

20th century
Innovative infrastructure

①
Stazione di Venezia Santa Lucia, Cannaregio
Terminal joy

Venice's train station is startling, a huge, truly modern building that penetrates this city's otherworldly sense of serenity. Completed in 1952 by engineer Paolo Perilli, the main station building and façade were the vision of the master of rationalist public buildings in the fascist era, Angiolo Mazzoni.

Its unflinching lines are all the more prominent thanks to the gleaming marble cladding – and the broad stairs to the entrance add extra drama. Inside, commercial necessities have partly spoiled that futuristic spirit.
Fondamenta Santa Lucia, 30100
veneziasantalucia.it

Venice
Design and architecture

② INPS Building, Dorsoduro
Official building

The regional seat of the National Social Provision Fund was finished in 1963 using designs by architect Virgilio Vallot. It forms part of what could be called a Venetian administrative district along the Rio Novo, dug in the 1930s to connect the Piazzale Roma to the central section of the Canal Grande (the Palazzo Rio Novo lies opposite).

Facing the canal, Vallot's building definitely suggests state officialdom; the brickwork patterns on the windowless walls on either side evoke Venetian decorative tradition. Do they hint at the layers of Byzantine bureaucracy within? *3519 Fondamenta Rio Nuovo, 30123 inps.it*

③ Casa Gardella alle Zattere, Dorsoduro
Best of both worlds

Designed by Ignazio Gardella in 1954, this apartment building is interesting because it came to symbolise a particularly Venetian solution to incorporating modern structures into the baffling historic urban fabric.

Using a palette of traditional materials and motifs, Gardella created a façade that is both contemporary in terms of postwar Italian apartment construction and respectful to a much-cherished waterfront context. The best way to appreciate this peculiar achievement? From the water.
Fondamenta Zattere allo Spirito Santo, 30123

④ Palazzo Rio Novo, Dorsoduro
Delicate genius

Built as the offices of the electricity board in 1960, the Palazzo Rio Novo has a complicated planning history so it's difficult to determine who it can be attributed to. Venetian architect Angelo Scattolin and Milanese contemporary Luigi Vietti were involved in plans that were drawn and redrawn for nearly a decade.

The resulting offices are attractive and unashamedly modernist. A three-storey block appears to float above the entrance, the supporting pillars ingeniously connected to the mass above. The delicate, geometrically inspired glazing is worth a second look.
3488 Calle Larga Ragusei, 30100

> **Floats our boat**
>
> Built for the 1979 Biennale Arte, Aldo Rossi's temporary Teatro del Mondo (Theatre of the World) was a 25-metre-tall floating structure that held 400 spectators. The yellow-and-green creation captured the imagination of architects and heralded the postmodern movement.

7 D Venice
Design and architecture

Face value — The modern façade offsets the buildings around it

⑤
Cassa di Risparmio, San Marco
Technically brilliant

The building designed to be the headquarters of the Venice savings bank was completed in 1970 to the designs of Angelo Scattolin and, most visibly, Italy's great structural engineer Pier Luigi Nervi. This boldly modern structure makes absolutely no effort to hide itself in the historic core that surrounds it – and for that reason many Venetians dislike it.

The critics have most likely never ventured inside because the main hall is one of Nervi's lesser-known technical marvels. The ceiling is composed of arch-shaped beams that fan out from the four supporting pillars, themselves things of sculptural beauty. All computer hardware was to be stored on the floors above, in case of flooding, although the two basement floors that reach nearly five metres below sea level were designed to be waterproof.
4216 Campo Manin, 30100
+39 041 529 1111

Up you go then, you'll look great up there

Venice
Design and architecture

Essential classics
Must-see marvels

①
Ca' d'Oro, Cannaregio
Go for gold

Once known as the Palazzo Santa Sofia, the Ca' d'Oro (House of Gold) got its nickname from its old gilt exterior – and it's still dazzling. A Canal Grande *des res par excellence*, it has to be seen from the water to make sense. It's a triumph of high Venetian gothic built between 1420 and 1436 by father-and-son architectural duo Giovanni and Bartolomeo Bon.
 The effect of the three levels of arches – which vary from simple to fancifully pointed – punctuated with quatrefoil windows is visually pleasing in the extreme.
3932 Calle Ca' d'Oro, 30126
+39 041 522 2349
cadoro.org

②
Santa Maria dei Derelitti, Castello
Healing power of music

Also known as the Ospedaletto (Little Hospital), the main church here was partly designed by Andrea Palladio. Sadly fire (note the still-charred wall) and water from frequent flooding mean it can be visited by appointment only.
 The Sala della Musica behind it was where patrons of the hospital would be sung to by a famed choir of young orphans, who would croon through trellised screens so they couldn't be seen. Now your eyes are free to wander and admire the architectural trickery visible in the frescoes.
6691 Calle della Barbaria delle Tole, 30122
+39 041 309 6605

Venice
Design and architecture

③

Ponte di Rialto, San Polo
Cross purposes

This site was, for a long period in Venetian history, the only way to cross the Canal Grande on foot. In 1854 the Ponte dell'Accademia was constructed and now the Rialto is one of four bridges to cross the city's watery artery.

After numerous collapses and fires on previous wooden structures, the authorities decided that a stone bridge should be constructed and opened the design up as a competition. Beating submissions by the likes of Palladio and Michelangelo, the appropriately named Swiss architect Antonio da Ponte came up with the winning concept and his vision was completed in 1591. The bridge is a true feat of renaissance engineering: the massive weight of its wide span is supported by 12,000 timber piles driven into the mud on both sides.
Sestiere San Polo, 30125

④

Palazzo Zenobio, Dorsoduro
Grand design

This baroque palazzo is exceptional for the full access it allows and the U-shaped layout holding an ample planted garden. The grandeur, vision and wealth of the Zenobio family from Verona is clear inside.

Construction started in 1690 to the designs of architect Antonio Gaspari and it remained in the Zenobios' hands until acquired by the Order of the Armenian Mekhitarist Brothers in 1850. The Armenian connection endures: today the palace houses the research centre for Armenian studies and an Armenian printing shop on the ground floor.
2597 Fondamenta del Soccorso, 30123
+39 041 522 8770

⑤

Scala Contarini del Bovolo, San Marco
High regard

This marvel shows the lengths (and heights) that Venetian families used to go to in order to outdo each other. The staircase is a cylindrical tower, 26 metres high, joined to the palazzo by way of a *loggia* (open passageway) at every level.

Built by Pietro Contarini in 1499 to the designs of an unknown architect, such was the success of the staircase that this branch of the noble Contarini family took its nickname ("del Bovolo", Venetian for "snail's shell") in its honour.
4299 Corte Contarini del Bovolo, 30124
+ 39 041 309 6605
scalacontarinidelbovolo.com

Scuola Grande di San Marco

The façade of this *scuola* combines classical and Byzantine influences. It has to be the world's most beautiful fully functioning hospital: note the boat ambulances moored along the western wall.
scuolagrandesanmarco.it

Venice
Design and architecture

Piazza San Marco

This piazza, which has to be the world's most famous square, never fails to impress. Allegedly Napoleon called it "the drawing room of Europe" and it's now synonymous with mass tourism. But what makes it so special?

The proportions of the main space, a trapezoid in shape, make for an optical wonder whichever way you look at it. The Basilica di San Marco, with its bewildering façade composed of great ogee arches and innumerable sculpted details, sets off the relatively austere straight lines of the apartments to the west, built to house the high offices of state from the 16th century onwards. Byzantine, gothic, renaissance and neoclassical styles collide and contradict to create a stupendous composition.

The current version of the famous Campanile was completed in 1912 to the exact specifications of the 1514 design (with the addition of a lift for modern convenience). The previous structure collapsed one morning in 1902 and miraculously, nobody was killed – apart from the caretaker's cat.

Churches
Religious experiences

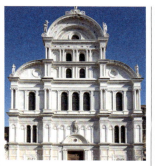

①
San Zaccaria, Castello
Changing face of architecture

Dedicated to Zechariah, the father of John the Baptist, this church dates from the 15th century. The magnificent façade very clearly expresses the metamorphosis in Venetian architecture at the time of construction; in 1458 architect Antonio Gambello started the church in a typically gothic style but higher up the abundant Corinthian columns and Roman arches are quintessentially renaissance. This is a reflection of both changing tastes and a change of architect: Mauro Codussi topped off the church some 50 years after Gambello started it.
4693 Campo San Zaccaria, 30122

②
San Giorgio Maggiore, Isola di San Giorgio Maggiore
Striking silhouette

A monastery was founded on this island adjacent to Giudecca in the 10th century. The current church was built to the designs of Andrea Palladio between 1566 and 1610 (he never lived to see it finished) and his genius was to create a strikingly classical façade in white marble, incorporating two pediments.

The classical minimalism continues inside, flooded by natural light. The silhouettes of Palladio's church and belltower now act as a dreamlike backdrop to the crowded main island of the city; a vista that inspired painters such as Monet.
Isola di San Giorgio Maggiore, 30100

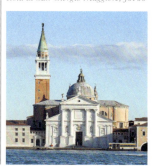

Venice
Design and architecture

③ I Gesuiti, Cannaregio
Opulent excess

If you can only visit the interior of one church in Venice then Santa Maria Assunta – or I Gesuiti, as it's more commonly known – should be it. The Jesuit order built the church in 1715; one theory goes that the confraternity, which was never particularly popular in Venice (hence the church's less-than-central location in Cannaregio) and had been briefly expelled in 1657, had to overcompensate with the decor in order to attract any visitors.

Virtually all the walls, columns, steps and floors are covered in what looks like opulently patterned fabric. This is in fact intarsia, or marble-inlay work, that was carried out with maniacal enthusiasm. WD Howells once described the interiors as "indescribably table-clothy", while Ruskin referred to I Gesuiti as "ridiculous". Whatever your opinion, this is definitely a must-see.

4885 Campo dei Gesuiti, 30100

Venice
Design and architecture

(4)
Santa Maria dei Miracoli, Cannaregio
Church of the impossible

There's something rather endearing about this little church from the 1480s. Its most striking feature is its unusually simple shape, a pleasingly naive interpretation of the Venetian renaissance. The form of the large semicircular pediment transcends into the barrel-vault ceiling inside.

Had it not been for dramatic intervention in the past century the church would not exist today. The high salt content of the marble cladding meant it was beginning to erode in the 1980s and, as the metal joists inside show, the church's design was structurally impossible.
6074 Campiello dei Miracoli, 30121

Unbuilt Venice

It comes as little surprise that architects the world over have long had a love affair with Venice. Its spellbinding urban juxtaposition, so unlike anything else, means that they jump at the chance to build in the city on the rare occasion that an opportunity arises.

However, desire is one thing – reality another. There is actually an entire unbuilt, unrealised Venice that can be found in the sketchbooks, plans and libraries of some of the world's greatest architects.

In 1953 Frank Lloyd Wright eagerly submitted plans for what would have been the Fondazione Masieri, on a very prominent site on the curve of the Canal Grande by the Ponte di Rialto. But the design, which recalled a vertical version of his Fallingwater house, was refused by the city on the grounds that it was not respectful enough of the neighbouring palazzo.

This culture of *"no, grazie"* continued to claim design victims, with subsequent acclaimed proposals by Le Corbusier (for a new hospital in 1964) and Louis Kahn (for a conference centre in 1969) never making it past the planning stage. Tough crowd.

Modern man

Appointed head of Works Management in 1931, Eugenio Miozzi oversaw the building of much of modern Venice, including the Ponte della Libertà road bridge beside the 1846 rail causeway. At 4km it was one of the longest structures of its time and yet was built in just two years.

Venice
D Design and architecture

Pavilions
International outposts

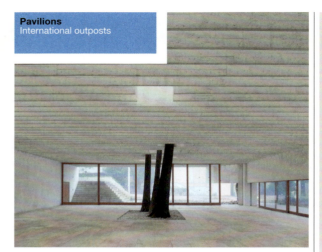

Biennale Architettura

The Biennale Architettura has occurred separately to the Biennale Arte since 1980, taking place throughout the summer on the even years of the calendar. The event summons the best and most pertinent projects and themes for a magnificent jamboree that, thanks to the recent directorship of architects such as Rem Koolhaas and Alejandro Aravena, is taken more seriously than ever.

As with the parallel art event, the Biennale Architettura profits from a unique set of built venues (and, of course, the city itself). The Arsenale complex hosts some of the most impressive shows, while the permanent gallery and exhibition spaces are some of the best examples of modern and contemporary architecture in the city. The Giardini area is home to the pavilions, an international menagerie of structures spanning the past 120 years of building styles.
labiennale.org

② Australian Pavilion, Castello
Think inside the box

Completed in 2015, Australia is the only pavilion in the Giardini to be built in the 21st century. Designed by Melbourne's respected architecture office Denton Corker Marshall, the basic idea for the structure was to insert a white box within a black box, with openings allowing the art inside to be seen from the outside.

The austere structure, clad with black granite, looms over the canal that runs through the Giardini and certainly gives the impression of boxiness. It is, however, both starkly contemporary and broodingly timeless, serving the Australian brand well.
Giardini della Biennale, 30122

① Nordic Pavilion, Castello
Scandinavian simplicity

This is probably one of the Giardini's most popular pavilions – and it's easy to see why. The Nordic countries share a pavilion (although the Danes have their own as well) so they were assigned a generous space.

It was designed by Pritzker prize-winning Norwegian architect Sverre Fehn in 1962 and stands as a tribute to the art of Nordic simplicity and respect for nature. The ceiling is composed of ultra-thin reinforced concrete girders that let the sun in between the gaps. Three pre-existing trees pierce the ceiling, making for a stunning permanent installation.
Giardini della Biennale, 30122

③ Israeli Pavilion, Castello
Clean slate

Israel's contribution to the Giardini's ensemble is small and easy to overlook but interesting nonetheless. The simple trapezoidal box was constructed in under a year in 1952, designed by one of the founding fathers of Israeli modernism, Zeev Rechter.

Rechter's sleek lines first graced Tel Aviv's famous Bauhaus-style White City and he went on to build some of young Israel's greatest public buildings. Featuring plain white walls on virtually all sides and ample exhibition space on its three levels, this pavilion masterfully achieves its role as a blank canvas.
Giardini della Biennale, 30122

Venice
Design and architecture

Visual identity
City quirks

1
Wellheads
Drink them in

There are approximately 230 stone wellheads dotted around the city and although none of the *pozzi* (wells) are still in use, their ubiquity and prominence tell an interesting history. With the city being built on small marshy islands in the middle of a saltwater lagoon, residents had no access to any naturally present fresh water. Large cisterns were therefore built under the city's *campi* to store rainwater collected at street level through metal or stone gratings.

The spots where the residents would draw the water, the wellheads, became focal points and over the years many were decorated and embellished. The renaissance gem of a *pozzo* in Campo Santi Giovanni e Paolo is (ahem) well worth a visit.

2
ACTV stations
Stop and look

There was a danger that the *fermate* – the modern floating cabins that act as stops for the vaporetto water-bus network – could spoil Venetian vistas. But thanks to a clean, uniform design by Venice-born Giulio Cittato, city transport consortium ACTV's stops add an urbane twist to the canal-side landscape.

Cittato studied and then worked under Massimo Vignelli, who designed the map and identity for the New York subway. This pedigree shows in the original use of the Helvetica typeface (later adapted to Arial) that is used for the station names and the ACTV logo itself.

Timeless design
Cittato's design has been used since 1977

③ Pointed arches
Peak your interest

If you had to pick one architectural feature to sum up Venice it might well be the pointed arch found on doors, windows and balconies across the city. Geographical and structural conditions conspired to make this distinctive Venetian device so prolific: as Europe's trading capital, Venice saw Byzantine (from Constantinople) and Arabic (from Moorish Spain) influences flood in and melt into the northern Italian gothic that was flourishing at the time.

Tracery (stone-and-metal work that surrounds glass windows) was also abundant so buildings are light for their size and have a delicacy that is quintessentially Venetian.

There's no point to this arch! But it's lovely all the same

Venice
Design and architecture

④
Gondolas and poles
Ferry appealing

They may be the most clichéd elements of the Venetian landscape but the city's famous graceful rowing boats are nonetheless a fundamental part of its urban visuals. A traditional gondola is made of up to eight different types of wood and has much symbolism attached to every element.

The six prongs on the strange F-shape at the prow represent the Venetian *sestieri*, with the prong facing the stern symbolising the island of Giudecca. The thousands of mooring poles are made of wood or concrete – and the attractive striped kind are usually found at the entrance to a palazzo or important building.

⑤
Stencilled street signs
Design directions

Given the city's convoluted labyrinth of streets and alleyways, it was essential that the Venetian signage system be one of the clearest and most easily interpreted in history (*see page 77*). The vast majority of the 4,000-plus signs are not objects themselves but rather consist of black lettering stencilled onto the white-painted rectangle that gives the signs their name: *nizioleti* (from the Venetian word for a small sheet).

The font used is sturdy yet delicate and has long been praised. In 2013 it was the basis of the visual style created for the Biennale Architettura by British designer John Morgan.

⑥
Chimneys
Catch the flues

There are estimated to be some 7,000 chimneys in Venice and while they vary in shape and size, their upturned cone-like heads – which resemble terracotta pots perched on columns – have been a familiar form on the Venetian cityscape for centuries.

The *camino* (chimney) features prominently in works by Tintoretto and Canaletto but it is perhaps Vittore Carpaccio's 1496 "Miracle of Santa Croce" that most strikingly depicts the scale and quantity of these flues. The enlarged brick chamber was devised to allow sparks to safely cool and not set light to any nearby wooden constructions.

Venice — Sport and fitness

Sport and fitness
— Healthy options

If you've come to Venice looking to get your heart rate up, prepare to be a little disappointed. This is a city where protracted sightseeing and marathon meals are the limit of the strenuous activities. Gyms are thin on the ground and the pavements of those narrow *calli* are hardly designed for pounding (that said, you'd be surprised how tiring crossing countless bridges can be).

Those determined to burn off their *cichèti* may have to settle for the fitness facilities in their hotel: the JW Marriott's offering tops our list. Otherwise most of Venice's leisure activities are water-based. Fancy yourself as a gondolier? Try your hand at *voga alla Veneta*. Or if you'd prefer something more familiar, hop in a kayak to cruise the canals.

Landlubbers will find our running routes useful: Venice may not be all that jogger-friendly but we did find a couple of places to pick up the pace. Or, if you'd rather relax, opt for a pamper with our spa and grooming options.

In and on the water
Splashing out

① Venice Kayak, Isola della Certosa
Glide the canals

What better way to get a duck's-eye view of Venice than from the seat of a kayak? Venetian Marco Ballarin and Dane René Seindal started Venice Kayak in 2011 and have been organising trips in the city's canals and the surrounding lagoon ever since.

From historical outings to expeditions to Burano, guides will accompany you to see the city from a different perspective. Tours usually take place from March to October and some paddling experience is preferred. The highly trained can also take winter trips.
Isola della Certosa, 30100
+ 39 346 477 1327
venicekayak.com

Venice
Sport and fitness

Lido

If the summer heat becomes unbearable, consider swapping Tintorettos and Titians for a tan and joining the troops of towel-toting Venetians on the vaporetto to Lido. This once-fabled Golden Isle faces the Adriatic and boasts clean water and sand that shelves away gently, allowing for safe swimming.

Once there, the simplest of many options is to walk straight down Granviale Santa Maria Elisabetta from the ferry stop to the beach. There are 11km of sand to explore, many of them fronted with rows of cabanas full of families who rent by the season. The more elegant hotels have private cabanas but the beach itself is public.

The more intrepid sun worshipper can pause at Lido on Bike near the vaporetto stop to rent wheels from €9 for the day. Once you're good to go, just pedal along the breakwater until you spot the most suitable stretch of sand.

Visitors in search of more strenuous exercise can find it in the form of tennis: the Ca' Del Moro club has four open-air clay courts and five covered options.
lidoonbike.it;
tennisclubcadelmoro.it

Piscina Sant'Alvise, Cannaregio
Get in lane

Located on the northern edge of Cannaregio, this 25-metre-long swimming pool is perfect for some serious lengths, while also having space for splashing about. The large bay windows look out onto the Parco di Villa Groggia, which is home to an amphitheatre dating back to the 1500s and a cast of crumbling statues.

Since this is a community pool, public swimming sessions take place throughout the day; check the website before donning your goggles. Sessions costs €6.50 for an adult and €4 for a child.
3163 Calle del Capitello, 30100
+39 041 524 0538
piscinasantalvise.it

Brussa Is Boat, Cannaregio
Deck yourself out

If you're one of those born sailors who can't be around large bodies of water without wanting to exercise your sea legs, you may find Venice something of a challenge. That said, why not think about hiring your own vessel?

Brussa Is Boat rents out typical Venetian flat-bottom *topette*, which hold up to six people and don't require a licence to drive (although you may be required to take a quick test before leaving the dock). And if you're stuck for ideas on where to drop anchor, see our best of the rest section (*page 126*).
331 Fondamenta Labia, 30121
+39 041 715 787
brussaisboat.it

Voga alla Veneta, Santa Croce
Old-school rowing

If you want to get acquainted with Venice's tradition of rowing, which is done standing up, learn from the professionals. But we're not talking gondoliers here, rather an all-female group of native and adopted Venetians who pass on the city's knowledge.

Away from the vaporettos, experienced rowers will teach you the art of *voga alla Veneta* (Venetian rowing). A private lesson for a group of up to four people lasts 90 minutes and takes place in a *batellina coda di gambero* (shrimp-tailed boat), once a common city craft (you can spot them in many of Canaletto's Venetian cityscapes).

Check out the *cichèti* option, which involves rowing to two *bàcari* to enjoy a glass of wine and a selection of the Venetian appetisers, or the evening row along the Canal Grande, when the sun starts to set and the traffic quiets down.
+39 347 725 0637
rowvenice.org

Lido is calling: time for some doggy paddle

123

Venice
Sport and fitness

Grooming
Spruce yourself up

①
Ca Bubi, San Polo
A cut above

The vintage interior of this tiny barbershop is a clue to the styles Mattia Palazzi specialises in: hairdos from the 1920s to the 1950s. Once a women's hairdresser, the moustachioed Palazzi started his own business in 2013 to recreate the atmosphere of a men's-only prohibition-era salon.
 Customers waiting their turn (there's only one cutting chair) are offered a beer or a nip of whiskey. Chit-chat soon ensues thanks to Palazzi's unspoken and unchanging rule that "what's said at the barber's stays at the barber's".
2433 Calle dell'Olio, 30125
+39 041 476 4256

②
Barbiere Davide Molin, San Marco
It's a snip

Look out for a thick white curtain embroidered with a pair of scissors, a razor and a comb, just a few steps away from the Chiesa di San Zaccaria: this is where Davide Molin has been cutting hair since he was 14. His father Gianfranco started the business in 1976 but this tiny Formica-clad establishment had been a barbershop since the early 20th century.
 Davide's father still occasionally jumps in to help with the finely executed and classic beard trims and haircuts, which have kept some faithful customers coming back for decades.
4716 C Campo San Provolo, 30122
+39 347 984 4894

③
Luca la Fenice, Cannaregio
Keeping trim

Venetian hairdresser Luca Bernardini started cutting hair in the 1980s and worked in both the Italian resort town of Riccione and London before returning to Venice to open his own salon. Today there are three branches in the city – in Cannaregio, Santa Croce and San Marco – and an outpost in Madrid.
 Each uses the founder's precise cutting technique to achieve bold cuts. Haircare products come courtesy of Bernardini's in-house line, which was created solely to be used in his salons but is now on sale.
2496 Fondamenta Misericordia, 30121
+39 041 721 088
lucalafenice.com

Spas
Just chill

①
Goco Spa, Sacca Sessola
Island retreat

Located on the island of Sacca Sessola, Venice's largest spa is part of the JW Marriott's sprawling island resort (*see page 22*). Alongside nine treatment rooms there's a sauna, a gym and a heated indoor pool that leads outdoors with views overlooking the lagoon. It may be out of the way but this well-designed spa, which is open to the public, is worth the trip.
Isola delle Rose, 30133
+39 041 852 1300
jwvenice.com/goco-spa-venice

②
Ai Reali Wellness Spa, Castello
Peaceful retreat

Ai Reali Wellness Spa is in the heart of the historical centre on a quiet canal (if you can believe such a thing exists). Set on the top floor of a renovated 17th-century palazzo, it's a good place to soothe any aches and pains with treatments influenced by Asian and Hawaiian traditions.
 Choose one of the full-body destressers, which include a head-to-toe hot-stone massage, or opt for something simple such as a manicure. The spa also boasts a Finnish sauna, a Turkish bath and a hydromassage pool.
5527 Campo della Fava, 30122
+39 041 241 5816
hotelaireali.com/reali_wellness

Venice
——— Sport and fitness S

Running routes
Hit the road

①
Giardini della Biennale
Go green

DISTANCE: 4km
GRADIENT: Flat
DIFFICULTY: Moderate
HIGHLIGHT: The gardens, as well as the fresh air along the waterfront
BEST TIME: Early evening
NEAREST VAPORETTO: San Marco San Zaccaria

Start by the stately *Palazzo Ducale*, with the water on your right. Cross the bridge, glancing left at the picture-perfect *Ponte dei Sospiri* (Bridge of Sighs), then go straight and cross the next bridge, choosing (as you can with most) to take the ramp or steps. Continue over the next four bridges, passing the Arsenale stop and the somewhat old-fashioned *Museo Storico Navale*, and you'll soon reach the lush Giardini della Biennale.
 Cross one more bridge then run round the gardens on the waterfront. Follow the gentle curve of the island, peeling right over the brick bridge to stick with the waterfront around the *Parco delle Rimembranze*. Head round the bend and loop back via the gardens, with the water now on your left. At the end take the left-hand diagonal path and cross the bridge. After rounding the corner go straight, turning right before the wall, then left again. Run through the arch, bearing right.
 Turn right, cross a stepless bridge and head towards the bronze *Monumento a Giuseppe Garibaldi*. Turn left onto Viale Giuseppe Garibaldi and then right down narrow Calle del Forno, crossing the bridge at the end. Follow the path into Campiello Tana and past the biennale entrance. At the water, bear right onto Fondamenta Arsenale, ending your run with a view of the sculpture-clad *Arsenale* entrance. Catch a vaporetto home from the Arsenale stop, cool down with a stroll along the water or run an extra 1km back to the start.

②
Zattere
Take in the sights

DISTANCE: 3km
GRADIENT: Flat
DIFFICULTY: Easy
HIGHLIGHT: Open views to Giudecca Island
BEST TIME: Early morning
NEAREST VAPORETTO: Ferrovia

Your run begins in the square in front of the squat *Stazione di Venezia Santa Lucia* (see page 110). Bear left and head to the Ponte degli Scalzi for a glorious view of the Canal Grande. Once you're on the other bank, head right past the great green dome of the Chiesa di San Simeone Piccolo, over a gentle bridge and all the way to the *Giardini Papadopoli*, one of Venice's few public parks. Turn left to follow the walls of the garden; on the Fondamenta Papadopoli you'll find an entrance if you want to take a loop around the park, otherwise keep going straight, past a bridge and under a short portico until you reach a boxy fascist-era government building.
 Cross the canal here and head straight following the Fondamenta Rio Nuovo; keep the canal on your left around the bend until you reach the gated *Palazzina Briati* (one of Università Ca' Foscari's buildings). From here cross the first bridge on your left that leads to the Chiesa di Santa Maria del Soccorso then bear right to follow the canal-side path until it opens up onto a small *campo*. Cross it diagonally for a short hop down a narrow *calle* and you'll be rewarded with views of Giudecca and the *Molino Stucky*. Now head right and follow the Zattere – looking up at the Chiesa dei Gesuati o Santa Maria del Rosario – crossing five bridges before you get to the tip of Dorsoduro, the *Punta della Dogana* (see page 94). Follow its perimeter to your left and you'll get to the *Basilica di Santa Maria della Salute* where you can finally catch your breath.

125

9 B Venice
Best of the rest

Best of the rest
— Get out of the city

01 02

Venice's crowds can test the patience of even the most tolerant traveller but, thankfully, relative solitude can be found just a hop, skip and a vaporetto ride from Piazza San Marco. The saltwater lagoon surrounding the city is home to more than 50 islands, ranging from the beachy to the bucolic. From restaurants and retail spots to bars and basilicas, here are 10 of our favourite boltholes and businesses, all found just a stone's throw from the throngs.

03

04

Venice
Best of the rest

01–02 Colourful houses of Burano
03 Burano's fishermen
04 Laundry day on Burano
05 Not your average airport shuttle
06 Rowing-club member
07 Dalla Lidia Merletti d'Arte lace shop
08 Making lace on Burano
09 Lagoon produce
10 Venini shopfront
11 Glassmaking on Murano

Address book

Venissa, Mazzorbo
A monastery in the 13th century, this chic retreat now houses a traditional osteria, a Michelin-starred restaurant, elegant guest rooms and a vineyard producing award-winning wines.
venissa.it

Residenze a Mazzorbo, Mazzorbo
This residential complex was designed by Genoese architect Giancarlo De Carlo. The hues may be traditional but the geometry is pure 1980s.

Trattoria al Gatto Nero, Burano
This Burano institution has been serving delicious seafood dishes under the watchful eye of chef Ruggero Bovo since 1965.
gattonero.com

Dalla Lidia Merletti d'Arte, Burano
Burano's oldest lace shop sells everything from household linen to baptism gowns.
dallalidia.com

Venini, Murano
Its glassware may be expensive but Venini's list of collaborators reads like a roll call of 20th-century design.
venini.com

9 Ⓑ Venice
Best of the rest

Wine and dine — Enjoy a meal at Venissa overlooking the vines

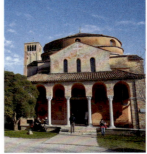

01 Vaporetto
02 Vineyard at Venissa
03 Locanda Cipriani
04 Venissa's Osteria Contemporanea
05 Aperitivo time
06 Tending Venissa's kitchen gardens
07–09 Torcello's Basilica di Santa Maria Assunta
10 Murano warehouses
11 Boat repairs
12 San Giorgio Maggiore
13 Le Stanze del Vetro
14–15 Beach o'clock on Lido

Venice
Best of the rest — B

10

11

12

13   14

15

Address book

Marina e Susanna Sent, Murano
This showroom and workshop displays elegant glass jewellery made by two Venetian sisters.
marinaesusannasent.com

Le Stanze del Vetro, Isola di San Giorgio Maggiore
Housed in the former boarding school of San Giorgio Maggiore, this contemporary exhibition space is dedicated to 20th and 21st-century glass.
lestanzedelvetro.org

Trattoria al Ponte di Borgo, Lido
A rustic restaurant known for its fish *cichèti* and for being a favourite of Corto Maltese's creator Hugo Pratt.
+39 041 770 090

Locanda Cipriani, Torcello
A tranquil and leafy *locanda* (hotel) in Torcello that was once the destination of choice for celebrities, royals and writers such as Ernest Hemingway.
locandacipriani.com

Basilica di Santa Maria Assunta, Torcello
The lagoon's oldest edifice dates back to 639 and is a beautiful example of Venetian-Byzantine architecture.
+39 041 730 084

Lagoon links

Route 12 departs from the Fondamente Nove and serves Murano, Mazzorbo, Torcello and Burano (in that order). There are at least two services every hour. Lido and San Giorgio Maggiore can be reached by multiple routes departing from San Marco San Zaccaria.
actv.avmspa.it

Venice Walks

Walks
— Find your own Venice

Now that we've rounded up our favourite places to eat, drink, shop and sleep, how about tackling the city area by area? Each of Venice's *sestieri* (sixths, or neighbourhoods) has a different vibe, from residential Cannaregio to spacious Castello and student-friendly Dorsoduro – and then there's Giudecca, a standalone island in itself. This is a city best explored by foot so hop to it: it's time to get up close and personal with Venice.

NEIGHBOURHOOD 01
Castello
Heritage wander

Taking its name from a fort built on the island of San Pietro di Castello, this neighbourhood is the largest in Venice – and the only one not to face onto the Canal Grande. It may have more of a working-class feel than some of the city's other *sestieri* but as the home of the biennale, Castello becomes a focus of attention during the summer months when the art and architecture aficionados descend.

Castello also has some of the city's most impressive historical drawcards, most obviously the 12th-century Arsenale, which spawned the city's naval industry. Now long idle, the shipbuilding yard can lay claim to being one of the first ever factories in the world (its name derives from the Turkish word for "place of production") and in its heyday workers could build a galley from start to finish in less than a day. The Ospedale della Pietà, meanwhile, was the church where Vivaldi taught, as well as the place where he composed several of his concertos.

But it's not all about sightseeing: Castello's *campi* are also perfect spots to indulge in a little people watching. Plus, their homely establishments provide some of the most appetising pastries and *cichèti* in Venice.

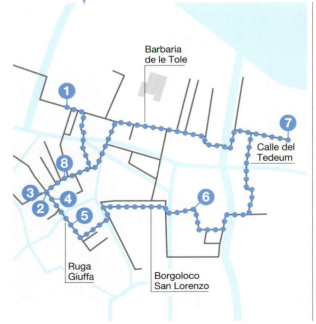

From churches to concept stores
Castello walk

Start your day the Italian way with some baked goods and a coffee at ❶ *Pasticceria Rosa Salva*, a small bakery that has been turning out fanciful traditional cakes and pastries since the late 19th century (its range for Carnevale is especially renowned). Elbow your way into a spot at the busy counter rather than opting for a table. Then exit right and take a right down Calle Vesier.

Venice Walks

Getting there

To reach Campo Santi Giovanni e Paolo take vaporetto lines 5.2 or 4.2 and disembark at Fondamente Nove. Walk south along the canal and then turn right onto Fondamenta Mendicanti. After a four-minute walk you'll reach the square.

Walk over the bridge and continue straight, turning right at the end. At the square you'll see your next stop, ❷ *Parrocchia Santa Maria Formosa*. Pop inside this 1492 church, which is guarded by comically hideous gargoyles on its exterior, to see Palma il Vecchio's portrayal of the voluptuous Saint Barbara.

Across from the entrance to the church you'll see a small shop, ❸ *Ferrari Bravo Cornici*, that has been selling picture frames since 1955. If you think your decor back home would benefit from an ornate gilt frame, this family-run business is the place to pick one up.

Next door you'll find another shop worth visiting: concept store ❹ *Tonolo Selezioni*. The space may be pint-sized but it stocks the very best from international design brands. Alongside an extensive selection of Freitag shoulder bags, you'll find Rimowa suitcases and Comme des Garçons wallets.

Continue along Ruga Giuffa, taking the first left. Soon you'll come to ❺ *Museo di Palazzo Grimani*, a spectacular building that was revamped in the 16th century to house the archeological collection of Giovanni Grimani (today it hosts temporary art exhibitions). Highlights include the lavish inlaid marble flooring and intricate stuccowork and frescos.

Retrace your steps back to the alley and turn left, then left again onto Calle di Mezzo. Cross the bridge, veer left and then right down Borgoloco San Lorenzo; when you hit the water cross the bridge. Continue to ❻ *Chiesa di San Lorenzo*, a church that dates back to the 9th century. It's said to have once been the resting place of Marco Polo but his remains were lost during the rebuild by Simone Sorella in the late 16th century.

Continue south on Calle San Lorenzo, following it around to the water and taking the bridge over to Corte Nuova Castello. Take the first left and then continue to the end of the alley. Turn right and then left again. Walk to the end and you'll hit ❼ *Chiesa di San Francesco della Vigna*, a renaissance-style church with two picturesque cloisters that are used as dramatic backdrops during the biennale.

Exit and walk down Calle San Francesco della Vigna, bearing left onto Ponte Fondamenta di Santa Giustina, to turn right over the bridge. Turn right at the end and left down Calle del Cafetier. You'll soon hit Calle de l'Ospealeto on your left, which becomes Calle Tetta. Cross two bridges then turn right onto Calle Longa Santa Maria Formosa. On your left is ❽ *Al Mascaron*, a homely osteria that's a favourite among locals. End your walk with some creamy *baccalà mantecato* (whipped salt cod) and a glass of chilled white wine.

Address book

01 Pasticceria Rosa Salva
6779 Campo Santi Giovanni e Paolo, 30122
+39 041 522 7949
rosasalva.it

02 Parrocchia Santa Maria Formosa
5263 Campo Santa Maria Formosa, 30100
+39 041 523 4645
santamariaformosa.it

03 Ferrari Bravo Cornici
5249A Campo Santa Maria Formosa, 30122
+39 041 523 6333

04 Tonolo Selezioni
5248A Campo Santa Maria Formosa, 30122
+39 041 241 1941
tonoloselezioni.com

05 Museo di Palazzo Grimani
4858 Ramo Grimani, 30122
+39 041 241 1507
palazzogrimani.org

06 Chiesa di San Lorenzo
Campo San Lorenzo, 30122

07 Chiesa di San Francesco della Vigna
2786 Campo San Francesco della Vigna, 30122
+39 041 520 6102

08 Al Mascaron
5225 Calle Longa Santa Maria Formosa, 30122
+39 041 522 5995
osteriamascaron.it

Venice Walks

NEIGHBOURHOOD 02
Cannaregio
Experience the everyday

Arching over the back of the Canal Grande like a sleeping cat, Cannaregio is Venice's second-largest and most-populated – yet often least-crowded – *sestiere*. Slip away from the tourist-choked artery that funnels visitors from the railway station to the Ponte di Rialto and you'll discover a different side to the city. Here souvenir shops give way to businesses that cater to the permanent residents – pet shops, florists and funeral parlours – quiet reminders that Venice is not simply a charming shell but a fully functioning city. It's home to a resilient population and some notable locals: Tintoretto, Titian and Marco Polo all hung their hats in this neighbourhood at one time or another.

The streets echo with Italian – or Venetian – as *nonnas* do their weekly shop and the city's stoic dogs are taken for their daily constitutional; you're more likely to share the coffee counter with a teacher or a tailor than a tour group. Even the urban-planning here is a little friendlier: the pavements are wider and the canals straighter, offering welcome relief from the claustrophobia that can set in across other parts of town.

Among Cannaregio's historical palazzos there are plenty of superlative places to eat and drink. And between stop-offs the district is best enjoyed with gelato in hand – so slow the pace and explore at your leisure; those osterias aren't going anywhere.

Going local
Cannaregio walk

Start your walk with a circuit of the atmospheric ❶ *Campo del Ghetto Nuovo*. As the heart of the very first Jewish ghetto, the area is still home to kosher cafés and bakeries.

Exit the square in the west corner and head down Calle Ghetto Vecchio until you reach ❷ *Antichità al Ghetto* on your right. This veritable Aladdin's cave sells everything from antique Murano glass, Venetian fabrics

and paintings to vintage jewellery and Jewish artefacts. Souvenirs purchased, carry on to the end of the street and pass through the archway, turning left onto Fondamenta Cannaregio. At the Ponte delle Guglie bear left onto the busy and rather uninspiring Rio Terà San Leonardo.

For a quick caffeine fix, dip into ❸ *Torrefazione Cannaregio* (*see page 42*), purveyor of arguably the best cappuccino in town. A few doors down is ❹ *Nave de Oro*, which sells *vino sfuso* – literally "unpackaged" wine – by the litre. Join the queue of locals waiting to fill their plastic bottles from the barrels of regional wine.

Continue up the street before turning right onto Calle del Pistor (perhaps nipping into ❺ *Nobile* to sample one of its sweet treats), then take Calle de l'Aseo across the canal and head right along Fondamenta Misericordia. Before long you'll pass costume emporium ❻ *Nicolao Atelier*. If you're in the market for a bead-encrusted bodice or a felt tricorn hat, Stefano Nicolao is your man (you're in

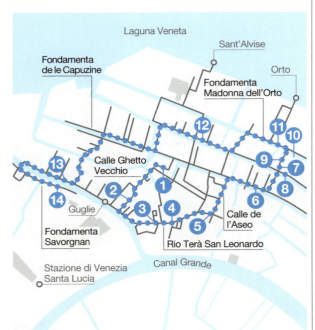

Venice
Walks

Address book

01 Campo del Ghetto Nuovo
Campo del Ghetto Nuovo, 30121

02 Antichità al Ghetto
1133/1134 Calle Ghetto Vecchio, 30121
+39 041 524 4592
antichitaalghetto.com

03 Torrefazione Cannaregio
1337 Rio Terà San Leonardo, 30121
torrefazionecannaregio.it

04 Nave de Oro
1370 Rio Terà San Leonardo, 30121
+39 041 719 695

05 Nobile
1818 Calle del Pistor, 30121
+39 041 720 731
pasticcerianobile.it

06 Nicolao Atelier
2590 Fondamenta Misericordia, 30121
+39 041 520 7051
nicolao.com

07 Osteria l'Orto dei Mori
3386 Campo dei Mori, 30121
+39 041 524 3677
osteriaortodeimori.com

08 Casa del Tintoretto
3399 Fondamenta dei Mori, 30121

09 Campo dei Mori
Campo dei Mori, 30121

10 Palazzo Mastelli
3401 Calle Tintoretto Cannaregio, 30121

11 Chiesa della Madonna dell'Orto
3512 Fondamenta Madonna dell'Orto, 30121
madonnadellorto.org

12 Osteria Anice Stellato
3272 Fondamenta de la Sensa, 30100
osterianicestellato.com

13 MQ10
1020 Fondamenta Cannaregio, 30100
+39 041 713 241

14 Al Parlamento
511 Fondamenta Savorgnan, 30121
+39 041 244 0214
alparlamento.it

safe hands: he made the costumes for the music video of Madonna's "Like a Virgin").

Carry on along the canal, turning left down Calle Larga and crossing the bridge at the end. This will lead you to the door of ❼ *Osteria l'Orto dei Mori*, where we recommend sampling one of Sicilian chef Lorenzo Cipolla's dishes.

A few doors down is the ❽ *Casa del Tintoretto*, once home to Jacopo Comin (or Tintoretto, as he's better known). Guarding the house you'll notice the statue of a turbaned merchant. This is one of the Mastelli brothers; you can find his two stone-faced siblings and servant in the neighbouring ❾ *Campo dei Mori*.

Continue through the square and over the bridge, turning back to admire their family home, ❿ *Palazzo Mastelli*, with its camel motif (*see page 73*). Then turn left onto Fondamenta Madonna dell'Orto in front of the handsome ⓫ *Chiesa della Madonna dell'Orto*. Pop inside to admire Signor Comin's handiwork – this was Tintoretto's parish church, home

Getting there

The closest vaporetto stops to the Campo del Ghetto Nuovo are Guglie on the Canale di Cannaregio (routes 4.1, 4.2, 5.1, 5.2 and A) and Sant'Alvise on the north shore (routes 4.1, 4.2, 5.1 and 5.2). By foot it's 10 minutes from the Stazione di Venezia Santa Lucia via Lista di Spagna.

to some of his best pieces and ultimately his final resting place.

Continue along the canal before turning left and crossing the bridge to take Calle Loredan onto Fondamenta de la Sensa. Turn right and keep going until you reach the cosy ⓬ *Osteria Anice Stellato* (*see page 37*), which serves some of the best *fritto misto* in town.

Carry on along Fondamenta de la Sensa, crossing the second bridge onto Calle Turlona, which you should follow to the end before turning right onto Fondamenta de le Capuzine. Again, take the second bridge onto the Calle del Batelo. Where it becomes Campiello Santo, bear left onto Fondamenta Battello. Cross the bridge onto Calle dei Vedei and follow it around the corner to Sotoportego dei Vedei and then Fondamenta Cannaregio.

It must be spritz o'clock by now so turn right and continue until you reach the white-walled ⓭ *MQ10*. If you have time for one last sundowner make your way to the opposite bank and join the trendy young things at ⓮ *Al Parlamento*, where the cocktails hit the spot.

133

NEIGHBOURHOOD 03
Dorsoduro
Making a scene

The most southerly of Venice's *sestieri*, Dorsoduro was once home to those who built and repaired the boats and gondolas that kept things running smoothly. Today there are still pockets of traditional industry – including Squero di San Trovaso, which is one of Venice's few thriving boatyards – but there are also plenty of small shops, cosy cafés, fantastic galleries and places to indulge in a glass of wine or two.

The Zattere promenade, which was built in 1516 as an unloading point for timber brought in from other regions, is chock-a-block with things to see. And while majestic churches are hardly an unfamiliar sight in the city, Dorsoduro is especially brimming with them, from the splendid dome of Santa Maria della Salute to the crumbling façade of San Nicolò dei Mendicoli and the masterpiece-filled Chiesa di San Sebastiano.

Thanks to the Università Iuav di Venezia, Dorsoduro is also buzzing with students and artists. This walk is full of design and architecture gems to admire against a blue sky but we'd recommend returning when the sun goes down: the bars in popular Campo Santa Margherita are some of the few places in Venice that you can let your hair down after dinner and enjoy a late-night drink.

Church service
Dorsoduro walk

Start at the ❶ *Basilica di Santa Maria della Salute*, one of Venice's largest churches. It was built in the 17th century after the Venetian Senate vowed to erect a church if the plague raging the city abated. (It did.) From there head west on Fondamenta Salute then turn right onto Calle del Bastion and walk until you reach the ❷ *Chiesa di San Gregorio*, a former church that's also been home to Benedictine monks, a metal-refining workshop and a hotel over the centuries.

From there continue down Calle del Bastion, cross the canal and turn left onto Campiello Barbaro. Follow it round to the right, then to the left at the end, where it becomes Fondamenta Venier dai Leon. After passing Collezione Peggy Guggenheim (*see page 90*) you'll see some shops: duck into ❸ *Marina e Susanna Sent SRL*, a small outpost of the Murano-based shop, to browse glass sculptures.

Carry on down the road until you reach Rio Terrà Foscarini and

Getting there

The nearest vaporetto stop to the walk's starting point is Salute. Only ACTV line 1 boats stop here but access is straightforward from both San Maria del Giglio and San Marco (Vallaresso) stops. From Salute it's a quick walk to Santa Maria della Salute (you can't miss it).

Venice
Walks

then turn right. Follow this road around the bend and glide by the popular Ponte dell'Accademia, carrying on down Campo Della Carità and passing the Gallerie dell'Accademia (*see page 92*). Turn right down Calle del Pistor and then left when you hit the canal. Cross the bridge opposite the always-buzzy Cantine del Vino già Schiavi (*see page 32*).

Turn left and walk for about a minute before arriving at the ❹ *Squero di San Trovaso*. This is the city's oldest boatyard, where

gondolas can still be built but are mostly repaired.

From there, cross the canal bridge to the south and turn left onto Calle Magazzen, followed by a quick right and then left onto the Fondamenta Zattere Al Ponte Longo. Take in the picture-perfect views across the canal of Giudecca, including the Molino Stucky – a former factory turned hotel. Stop and admire the ❺ *Adriatica Società di Navigazione* building. Once the Venetian headquarters of a large shipping and cruise company,

the building's pretty façade still boasts the glittering signage of its former heyday.

Once you get to the end of the promenade, bear right onto Calle del Vento and then left onto Fondamenta de San Basegio. When you reach the canal turn right and cross the second bridge you come across. You'll arrive at the ❻ *Chiesa di San Sebastiano*, the inside of which is decorated with an array of artwork by Paolo Veronese; this is also where the artist is buried.

Just beyond the church, head north up Campiello Fondamenta San Sebastiano and left along the canal to the ❼ *Chiesa dell'Angelo Raffaele*. Thought to be one of the city's oldest churches, some believe it was built as early as 416. By now you'll certainly be in need of a caffeine hit so cross the bridge, hang a left and pop into ❽ *Caconero* for a coffee and some tasty *cichèti*.

Once you're sated, carry on down the road until you reach Calle Rielo Dorsoduro, taking a left when you reach the canal again. Here you'll discover ❾ *San Nicolò dei Mendicoli*, a small, crumbling church – no photos allowed – that was the setting of many scenes in the 1973 film *Don't Look Now*.

Continue down the road and turn left. Cross the bridge and you'll come to the ❿ *Università Iuav di Venezia*, which today produces some of the country's most talented design students and apprentices.

Address book

01 **Basilica di Santa Maria della Salute**
1 Campo della Salute, 30123
basilicasalutevenezia.it

02 **Chiesa di San Gregorio**
Calle Due Mori, 30123

03 **Marina e Susanna Sent SRL**
681 Campo San Vio, 30123
+39 041 520 8136
marinaesusannasent.com

04 **Squero di San Trovaso**
1097 Fondamenta Bonlini, 30123

05 **Adriatica Società di Navigazione**
Fondamenta Zattere Al Ponte Longo, 30123

06 **Chiesa di San Sebastiano**
Campo San Sebastiano, 30123
+39 041 275 0462

07 **Chiesa dell'Angelo Raffaele**
1721 Campo Anzolo Raffaele, 30123
+39 041 522 8548

08 **Caconero**
2344 Fondamenta Barbarigo, 30123
caconero.it

09 **San Nicolò dei Mendicoli**
1907 Campo San Nicolò, 30123
+39 041 275 0382

10 **Università Iuav di Venezia**
191 Campo Tolentini, 30135
+39 041 257 1644
iuav.it/homepage

NEIGHBOURHOOD 04
Giudecca
Island living

Cosying up to the south side of the main island, Giudecca is a slither of land originally called Spinalonga (Long Spine) on account of its curvilinear shape. In fact it's part of Dorsoduro and made up of eight mini islands threaded together by canals and bridges. Weave your way through them and you'll see why some call this the "real Venice" due to the distinct lack of tourists.

It began as a fishing village in about 500AD and later became the rural playground of the elite, a jumble of palazzos and gardens. Its name references the *giudicati* (judged ones): roguish aristocrats who were banished here from the mainland in the 9th century. Today it's a happy mix of fishermen and celebrities.

An unlikely pairing also comes in the form of its architecture, a combination of classical and industrial buildings. In the 19th century, companies transferred their operations here to make use of the space and access to the sea; one example was Giovanni Stucky's flour mill, now the Hilton Molino Stucky.

When the mill closed in 1955 the island fell into disrepair but now it's thriving once more, especially its art scene. Independent galleries are always open and on best form during the biennale (call ahead if visiting off season). For that reason this walk is best suited to the summer months. Plus, a stroll along the waterfront is most enjoyable when the sun is shining.

Culture and calm
Giudecca walk

After hopping off the vaporetto at Palanca turn left and nip along Fondamenta Sant'Eufemia for a pre-walk pit-stop at ❶ *Majer*. Energise yourself with a coffee then head back to the vaporetto stop.

Opposite Palanca is ❷ *Studio Sant'Eufemia*, a gallery that displays paintings and drawings of the city by Venetian artist Laura Lo Verso. Admire the charming cityscapes and pick up a postcard or two.

Continue along Fondamenta Sant'Eufemia with the water on your right and cross the first bridge you come to. You'll spy the Fortuny Showroom and Factory ahead but before you reach it, duck under the archway to your left. This industrial complex – now home to a clutch of cutting-edge galleries and studios – used to contain a network of breweries. A left at the end followed by a right will lead you to ❸ *Galleria Michela Rizzo*: do as the gold sign says and ring the bell. Michela Rizzo's commercial-art gallery, which opened on the mainland in 2004 and hosts emerging international artists, moved to Giudecca in 2013.

Turn back and pop next door to another gallery, ❹ *Spazio Punch*, which opened in the former warehouse of the Dreher brewery in 2011 and is co-directed by Augusto Maurandi and Saul Marcadent. It's a venue for fashion, architecture, publishing and art and, in a nod to its roots, also produces Ex B (*see page 64*), an organic craft beer.

Ask Maurandi to show you his workshop then leave through the

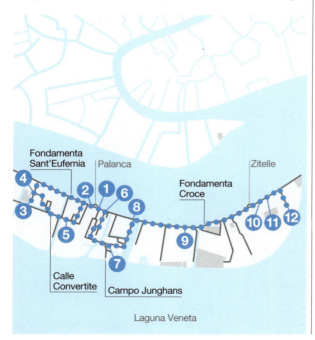

Venice
—— Walks

Address book

01 Majer
461 Fondamenta
Sant'Eufemia, 30135
+39 041 521 1162
majer.it

02 Studio Sant'Eufemia
597 Fondamenta
Sant'Eufemia, 30133
+39 041 241 0831
eufemiastudio.it

03 Galleria Michela Rizzo
800Q Isola della Giudecca,
30133
+39 041 839 1711
galleriamichelarizzo.net

04 Spazio Punch
800O Isola della Giudecca,
30133
spaziopunch.com

05 Fondazione Archivio Luigi Nono
619-621 Calle Cosmo,
30123
+39 041 520 9713

06 La Palanca
448 Fondamenta Ponte
Piccolo, 30133
+39 041 528 7719

07 Teatro Junghans
Campo Junghans, 30133
+39 041 241 1974
accademiateatraleveneta.com/teatro-junghans

08 Andrea Tardini Gallery
282 Fondamenta Ponte
Lungo, 30133
+39 041 099 1079
andreatardinigallery.com

09 Chiesa del Santissimo Redentore
1 Campo Santissimo
Redentore, 30133
+39 041 275 0462

10 Tre Oci
43 Fondamenta delle
Zitelle, 30133
+39 041 241 2332
treoci.org

11 Le Zitelle
32 Fondamenta delle
Zitelle, 30133
+39 041 532 2920

12 Belmond Hotel Cipriani
10 Fondamenta San
Giovanni, 30133
+39 041 240 801
belmond.com

back entrance, crossing the first bridge you come to and turning left onto Calle Convertite. Continue over a second bridge, past a church and on your right you'll see the arched entrance to ⑤ *Fondazione Archivio Luigi Nono*; once inside it's the first door on your left. This archive is dedicated to the Venetian avant garde composer and directed by his widow.

Turn right as you leave, then left onto Calle del Pistor, which leads back to the waterfront. Take a right and continue back past Palanca to

Getting there

From the mainland, Giudecca is a three-minute boat ride (routes 2, 4.1 and N) across the Canale della Giudecca. To get to Palanca and the start of the walk take line 2 from Zattere; the word *palanca* refers to the name of the coin that was once needed to pay for the ride.

⑥ *La Palanca*, a neighbourhood bar that's perfect for a laidback lunch. If it's warm sit outside and soak up the view as you enjoy a plate of cuttlefish-ink risotto.

Once you've had your fill, head down Calle dell'Olio. At the end bear left onto Calle Scuola, crossing the bridge into Campo Junghans (*see page 105*), home to ⑦ *Teatro Junghans*. This theatre was first used as the Junghans watch-making factory and then to store bomb parts in the Second World War. At the end of Calle Scuola turn left onto Calle de le Erbe, then right when you reach the waterfront. On the corner is ⑧ *Andrea Tardini Gallery*, opened in 2015 as a space for both Venetian and international artists.

Continue over the bridge to ⑨ *Chiesa del Santissimo Redentore*, designed by Andrea Palladio in the style of ancient Roman architecture. The church was built between 1577 and 1592 to celebrate the end of the 1576 plague, which wiped out a third of the city's population.

Over the next bridge is ⑩ *Tre Oci* (*see page 93*) – a photography museum with a striking neo-gothic façade – and just beyond that ⑪ *Le Zitelle*. Originally attached to a foundling hospital for girls, the latter too was designed by Palladio. Visiting is appointment-only but anyone can admire the classical architecture.

If you're ready to return to the mainland walk back to the Zitelle stop and catch a vaporetto to San Zaccaria. Or continue along Fondamenta San Giovanni and take the first right to ⑫ *Belmond Hotel Cipriani*. Bellini, anyone?

Venice
Resources

Resources
— Inside knowledge

So now you know where to find the best backstreet wine bars, which commercial-art galleries you should call on and why the smaller islands are worth visiting. Aside from when you need to venture across the glistening lagoon, we suggest you walk everywhere; the crooked streets can be tricky to navigate but getting lost isn't a bad way to get to know the city. In this section we've also gone through the nitty gritty of getting here from two nearby airports.

You'll find a listing of our favourite events, from the film festival to the biennale. There's also a handful of useful Venetian words and a soundtrack to inspire you as you explore. We've come up with a mix of fair and wet-weather activities too so that no matter when you visit, you'll find myriad ways to enjoy the city.

Transport
Get around town

01 **On foot:** Walking is the best way to get to grips with this labyrinth of a city. Just be aware of the rules of the road (*see page 14*).
02 **Vaporetto:** When it comes to going further afield, vaporettos are the easiest and most affordable option, ferrying visitors along the main canals and to the islands around the lagoon. Regular services run from about 05.00 to midnight, after which there are night services. Tickets are available at *tabacchi* and vaporetto stops, while tourist travel cards can be bought at vaporetto ticket offices or online. A ticket valid for 75 minutes costs €7.50.
actv.avmspa.it
03 **Gondola:** The quintessential Venetian ride costs about €90 for 40 minutes. Some say it's worth it, others disagree; we'll leave it to you to decide.
gondolavenezia.it
04 **Traghetto:** If you're far from one of the four bridges that cross the Canal Grande your best bet is a *traghetto* (ferry), a shabby gondola of sorts that's rowed back and forth across the main drag at seven points between the train station and Piazza San Marco. A quick and cheap (€2 a head) alternative to a gondola.
05 **Water taxi:** A pricey option but handy when you're in a hurry. Rates start at €13 plus €2 per minute; there are extra charges for additional luggage and groups of more than five people, plus €10 for night trips and €6 if called to a hotel. There are pick-up points at Piazzale Roma and the train station, as well as by the Rialto and San Marco Vallaresso vaporetto stops but it's more reliable to book.
motoscafivenezia.it

Flights
Making an entrance

01 **Venezia Marco Polo:** Venice's official airport, 10km from the city, is easily the most convenient option. There are two bus services to Piazzale Roma, both of which cost €8 one-way and take 30 minutes. The Alilaguna boat service drops you at major ferry stops around the lagoon; it takes up to 90 minutes, costs €15 and is practical if you're heading to one of the smaller islands. A taxi costs €40 and takes 20 minutes; or, if you really want to arrive in style, a 30-minute water taxi costs €100.
02 **Venezia Treviso-Sant'Angelo:** Treviso airport is 35km from Venice; a bus to Piazzale Roma costs €12 and takes up to 90 minutes. Or take a 20-minute bus to Treviso Centrale train station and catch a 35-minute train.

Vocabulary
Local lingo

The Venetian dialect, also known in the native tongue as the *dialeto del mar* (dialect of the sea), was the official language of the Venetian republic for almost 1,000 years and is still widely spoken among locals today. It's typified by colourful expressions, a nasal delivery and the slurring of words.

01 **Ostregheta!** Goodness!
02 **Bàcaro:** Wine bar
03 **Ombra:** Glass of wine
04 **Ciapàr:** To take
05 **Varda:** Look
06 **Cichèti:** Small snacks
07 **Pantegana:** Big rat found in Venice's canals
08 **Schei:** Money
09 **Cagnàra:** Din
10 **Ciò:** Of course

138

Venice
Resources

Soundtrack to the city
Five top tunes

01 Antonio Vivaldi, 'Le Quattro Stagioni': Venice-born Vivaldi's set of four violin concertos is often playing in the city's theatres.
02 Francesco Guccini, 'Venezia': A melancholy portrait of *la dolce ossessione* (that sweet obsession) that tourists have with Venice – and the effect that it has had on the city.
03 Pitura Freska, 'Papa Nero': All-Venetian Reggae band Pitura Freska (Wet Paint) shot to fame in the 1990s with their witty Venetian-dialect songs about sex and cannabis.
04 Franco Battiato, 'Venezia-Istanbul': Italian singer-songwriter Franco Battiato's lyrics speak of Venice's similarity to the East.
05 Claudio Monteverdi, 'L'Orfeo': A fine opera from the Venetian composer.

Best events
What to see

01 Carnevale, Piazza San Marco: This flamboyant two-week festival from the Middle Ages came into its own in the 18th century as an outlet for all that was prohibited by the doge.
January/February, carnevale.venezia.it
02 Vogalonga, Bacino di San Marco: A colourful 30km regatta that sees amateurs race around the lagoon and the city's two main canals in protest at motorboats.
May/June, vogalonga.com
03 Festa della Sensa, San Nicolò al Lido & Bacino di San Marco: In memory of Venice's symbolic marriage to the sea, the Feast of the Ascension sees the mayor board the state barge and throw a laurel wreath overboard. A regatta follows.
May

04 La Biennale, Giardini and Arsenale: A major international showcase that injects the city with contemporary art and architecture – and those who follow. Held in locations across the city but based primarily in and around the Giardini and Arsenale.
Art: May to November (odd years). Architecture: May to November (even years), labiennale.org
05 Festa del Redentore, Bacino di San Marco and Canale della Giudecca: This annual celebration in the Venetian calendar began after the end of a plague epidemic in 1576. Festivities, including a picnic and show-stopping fireworks, are followed by a pilgrimage.
July
06 Venezia Jazz Festival, Various venues: Jazz takes over the city's open spaces, theatres and museums.
July, venetojazz.com
07 Mostra Internazionale d'Arte Cinematografica, Lido: Venice's international film festival is a chance to see some of the industry's best talent, as well as a red carpet full of fashionistas.
August to September, labiennale.org
08 Regata Storica, Canal Grande: The main event in the city's rowing calendar, featuring four races and a procession of ornate boats and costumed characters.
September, regatastoricavenezia.it
09 Venice Marathon, Various venues: Runners start in Stra, east of Padua, and follow the Riviera del Brenta to Venice before finishing at the Riva dei Sette Martiri.
October, venicemarathon.it
10 Festa della Madonna della Salute, Basilica di Santa Maria della Salute: A procession to the church to celebrate *salute* (good health). Cakes, candyfloss and *castradina* (cabbage-and-mutton stew) included.
November

Rainy days
Weather-proof activities

01 Hot chocolate: The *cioccolata calda* in Venice is rich and velvety and has been prized since the 18th century, when Caffè Florian served it to Casanova. Head there for a particularly decadent cup or, for a less touristy experience, pop into one of the city's *pasticceria* (pastry shops).
caffeflorian.com
02 Churches: Suitable when the heavens open, Venice is brimming with grandiose churches piled high with paintings and sculptures by Venetian masters.
03 Visit a museum: Museo Correr in Piazza San Marco will give you a good insight into the art and history of the city – and keep you busy for a suitably long time on a rainy day.
correr.visitmuve.it

Sunny days
The great outdoors

01 Giardini della Biennale: This vast public park in Castello was laid out by order of Napoleon in the 19th century and includes lakes, playgrounds and tree-lined alleyways. A relaxing option – except during biennale.
02 Visit an island: Hop on a vaporetto and take a tour of some of the smaller islands. Lido offers sandy shores and a place to ride a bike, while Torcello is appealingly quiet and has a cathedral that should be seen by everyone who is interested in Venetian-Byzantine art.
03 Eat and drink alfresco: Make like the locals and head to a *bàcaro*. Order a glass of Italian wine and a selection of *cichèti* then head outside, prop yourself up against a wall and soak up the rays.

139

Venice
About Monocle

About Monocle
—— Step inside

London HQ
Our editorial office is in Marylebone

In 2007, Monocle was launched as a monthly magazine briefing on global affairs, business, culture, design and much more. We believed there was a globally minded audience of readers who were hungry for opportunities and experiences beyond their national borders.

Today Monocle is a complete media brand with print, audio and online elements – not to mention our expanding network of shops and cafés. Besides our London HQ we have seven international bureaux in New York, Toronto, Istanbul, Singapore, Tokyo, Zürich and Hong Kong. We continue to grow and flourish and at our core is the simple belief that there will always be a place for a print brand that is committed to telling fresh stories and sending photographers on assignments. It's also a case of knowing that our success is all down to the readers, advertisers and collaborators who have supported us along the way.

1
International bureaux
Boots on the ground

We have an HQ in London and call upon firsthand reports from our contributors in more than 35 cities around the world. We also have seven international bureaux. For this travel guide, MONOCLE reporters Chloë Ashby, Joe Pickard, Chiara Rimella and Megan Gibson decamped to Venice to explore all that it has to offer. They also called on the assistance of writers in Italy, as well as our correspondents David Plaisant and Ivan Carvalho, to ensure that we have covered the best in retail, food, hospitality and entertainment. The aim is to make you, the reader, feel like a local when visiting La Serenissima.

2
Online
Digital delivery

We have a dynamic website: monocle.com. As well as being the place to hear our radio station, Monocle 24, the site presents our films, which are beautifully shot and edited by our in-house team and provide a fresh perspective on our stories. Check out the films celebrating the cities that make up our Travel Guide Series before you explore the rest of the site.

3
Retail and cafés
Food for thought

Via our shops in Hong Kong, Toronto, New York, Tokyo, London and Singapore we sell products that cater to our readers' tastes and are produced in collaboration with brands we believe in. We also have cafés in Tokyo and London. And if you are in the UK capital visit the Kioskafé in Paddington, which combines good coffee and great reads.

Venice
— About Monocle

④
Print
Committed to the page

MONOCLE is published 10 times a year. We have stayed loyal to our belief in quality print with two extra seasonal publications: THE FORECAST, packed with key insights into the year ahead, and THE ESCAPIST, our summer travel-minded magazine. To sign up visit *monocle.com/subscribe*. Since 2013 we have also been publishing books, like this one, in partnership with Gestalten.

⑤
Radio
Sound approach

Monocle 24 is our round-the-clock radio station that was launched in 2011. It delivers global news and shows covering foreign affairs, urbanism, business, culture, food and drink, design and print media. When you find yourself in Venice tune into *The Globalist*, our morning news programme that is the perfect way to start the day in Europe. We also have a playlist to accompany you day and night, regularly assisted by live band sessions that are hosted at our Midori House headquarters in London. You can listen live or download any of our shows from *monocle.com*, iTunes or SoundCloud.

Priority service
—
Subscribers save 10 per cent in our online shop

Choose your package

Premium one year
12 × issues
+ Porter Sub Club bag

One year
12 × issues
+ Monocle Voyage tote bag

Six months
6 × issues

Join the club

01
Subscribe to Monocle
A subscription is a simple way to make sure that you never miss an issue – and you'll enjoy many additional benefits.

02
Be in the know
Our subscribers have exclusive access to the entire Monocle archive and priority access to selected product collaborations at *monocle.com*.

03
Stay in the loop
Subscription copies are delivered to your door at no extra cost no matter where you are in the world. We also offer an auto-renewal service to ensure that you never miss an issue.

04
And there's more…
Subscribers benefit from a 10 per cent discount at all Monocle shops, including online, and receive exclusive offers and invitations to events around the world.

Venice
Acknowledgements

Writers
Chloë Ashby
Alex Bamji
Aaron Betsky
Beatrice Carmi
Ivan Carvalho
Jenny Condie
Tom Furse
Megan Gibson
Naomi Joseph
Daphne Karnezis
Pete Kempshall
Gino Macropodio
Laura Morelli
Valeria Necchio
Russell Norman
Joe Pickard
David Plaisant
Amy Richardson
Chiara Rimella
Ben Rylan
James Taylor-Foster
Erla Zwingle

Chief photographer
James Mollison

Still life
David Sykes

Images
Alamy
Andrea Avezzù
Marta Buso
Francesco Castagna
Alessandra Chemollo
Michele Crosera
Sverre Fehn
Matteo de Fina
Enrico Fiorese
La Fenice Press Office
Valeria Necchio
PA Images
Marco Picci
Venissa
Simon Watson

Illustrators
Satoshi Hashimoto
Ceylan Sahin
Tokuma

Monocle
EDITOR IN CHIEF AND CHAIRMAN
Tyler Brûlé
EDITOR
Andrew Tuck
CREATIVE DIRECTOR
Richard Spencer Powell

Venice
Acknowledgements

The Monocle Travel Guide Series: Venice
GUIDE EDITORS
Chloë Ashby
Joe Pickard
ASSOCIATE GUIDE EDITORS
Megan Gibson
Chiara Rimella
PHOTO EDITOR
Victoria Cagol

The Monocle Travel Guide Series
SERIES EDITOR
Joe Pickard
ASSOCIATE EDITOR
Chloë Ashby
ASSISTANT EDITOR
Mikaela Aitken
RESEARCHER
Melkon Charchoglyan
DESIGNERS
Loi Xuan Ly
Jay Yeo
PHOTO EDITORS
Matthew Beaman
Victoria Cagol
Shin Miura

PRODUCTION
Jacqueline Deacon
Dan Poole
Rachel Kurzfield
Sean McGeady
Sonia Zhuravlyova

CHAPTER EDITING

Need to know
Chloë Ashby

Hotels
Megan Gibson

Food and drink
Valeria Necchio

Retail
Chiara Rimella

Things we'd buy
Joe Pickard
Chiara Rimella

Essays
Chloë Ashby

Culture
Chloë Ashby

Design and architecture
David Plaisant

Sport and fitness
Joe Pickard

Best of the rest
Joe Pickard

Walks
Joe Pickard

Resources
Chloë Ashby

Research
Beatrice Carmi
Melkon Charchoglyan
Mikaela Aitken
Naomi Joseph
Ceinwen Thomas
Zayana Zulkiflee

Special thanks
Azienda Veneziana della Mobilità Spa
Kathy Ball
Matteo Bisol
Paul Fairclough
Kaoru Ishikawa
Pete Kempshall
Bill Leuty
Amy Richardson

Venice
Index

A

A plus A Gallery, *San Marco* 98
Acqua e Mais, *San Polo* 35
Ai Do Draghi, *Dorsoduro* 43
Ai Reali Wellness Spa,
  Castello 124
Al Covo, *Castello* 27
Al Duca d'Aosta, *San Marco* 47
Al Mercà, *San Polo* 42
Al Ponte Antico, *Cannaregio* 23
Al Timon, *Cannaregio* 32
All'Arco, *San Polo* 35
Alma Zevi, *San Marco* 99
Altrove, *San Polo* 51
Aman Venice, *San Marco* 18 – 19
Annelie, *Dorsoduro* 56
Antiche Carampane, *San Polo* 31
Arzanà, *Cannaregio* 95
Aula Mario Baratto,
  Dorsoduro 109
Australian Pavilion, *Castello* 118

B

Bacareto Da Lele, *Santa Croce* 33
Bar alla Toletta, *Dorsoduro* 37
Barbiere Davide Molin,
  San Marco 124
Barena, *San Marco* 50
Basilica di Santa Maria Assunta,
  Torcello 129
Basilica di Santa Maria Gloriosa
  dei Frari, *San Polo* 90
Bauer Venezia, *San Marco* 17
Best of the rest 126 – 129
Biblioteca della Biennale,
  Castello 100
Biblioteche della Fondazione
  Giorgio Cini, *Isola di San
  Giorgio Maggiore* 101
Biennale, La, *citywide* 97, 118
Birraria La Corte, *San Polo* 29
Bollicine, *Dorsoduro* 43
Boselli, *Dorsoduro* 52
Bottega del Tintoretto,
  Cannaregio 100
Bottega Veneta, *San Marco* 51
Bruno with Motto,
  Dorsoduro 60 – 61
Brussa Is Boat, *Cannaregio* 123
Buosi Successori,
  San Marco 48
Burano 127

C

Ca Bubi, *San Polo* 124
Ca' d'Oro, *Cannaregio* 113
Cà' d'Oro Alla Vedova,
  Cannaregio 31
Ca' Macana, *Dorsoduro* 56
Ca Maria Adele, *Dorsoduro* 25
Ca' Pesaro, *San Polo* 93
Ca' Rezzonico, *Dorsoduro* 94
Caffè Florian, *San Marco* 41

Caffè Girani, *Castello* 40
Cafoscarina, *Dorsoduro* 61
Cannaregio 23, 31, 32, 34, 37, 38,
  40, 42, 43, 45, 46, 56, 58, 90,
  95, 100, 102, 104, 110, 113,
  116, 117, 123, 124, 132 – 133
Cantina Do Mori, *San Polo* 33
Cantine del Vino già Schiavi,
  Dorsoduro 32
Carlo Moretti, *Murano* 53
Casa del Parmigiano, *San Polo* 38
Casa Flora, *San Marco* 21
Casa Gardella alle Zattere,
  Dorsoduro 111
Cassa di Risparmio,
  San Marco 112
Castello 26, 27, 28, 30, 36, 39,
  40, 44, 60, 61, 100, 102, 107,
  113, 114, 115, 118, 124, 125,
  130 – 131
Chet Bar, *Dorsoduro* 43
Chiarastella Cattana,
  San Marco 52
Chiesa della Madonna dell'Orto,
  Cannaregio 90
Chiesa di San Sebastiano,
  Dorsoduro 90
Cima Rosa, *Santa Croce* 16
Cimiterio di San Michele,
  San Michele 106
Collezione Peggy Guggenheim,
  Dorsoduro 90 – 91
Corte Sconta, *Castello* 36
CoVino, *Castello* 26

D

Dal Nono Colussi, *Dorsoduro* 39
Dalla Lidia Merletti d'Arte,
  Burano 127
Dorsoduro 25, 29, 30, 32, 37, 38,
  39, 43, 45, 52, 53, 56, 57, 58,
  60 – 61, 90 – 91, 92, 94 – 95,
  98, 101, 102, 109, 111, 114,
  134 – 135

E

El Sbarlefo San Pantalon,
  Dorsoduro 45
Enoiteca Mascareta, *Castello* 44
Espace Louis Vuitton Venezia,
  San Marco 96
Essays 65 – 88
Estro, *Dorsoduro* 30

F

Fallani, *Cannaregio* 58
Floating greengrocers, *citywide* 33
Fondazione Emilio e Annabiana
  Vedova, *Dorsoduro* 92
Fondazione Prada,
  Santa Croce 94
Fondazione Querini Stampalia,
  Castello 107

Former Junghans area,
  Giudecca 105
Franco Puppato, *San Marco* 47

G

G Benevento, *Cannaregio* 46
Gabriele Gmeiner, *San Polo* 55
Galerie Bordas, *San Marco* 97
Gallerie dell'Accademia,
  Dorsoduro 92
Gelateria il Doge, *Dorsoduro*
  and *San Polo* 39
Gelateria Nico, *Dorsoduro* 39
Gelatoteca Suso, *San Marco* 39
Gianni Basso Stampatore,
  Cannaregio 56
Giardini della Biennale,
  Castello 125
Gilberto Penzo, *San Polo* 59
Giorgio Mastinu Fine Art,
  San Marco 99
Giudecca 33, 43, 90, 93, 105,
  136 – 137
Giuliana Longo, *San Marco* 57
Goco Spa, *Sacca Sessola* 124
Godi Fiorenza, *San Marco* 50
Goppion Caffetteria,
  Cannaregio 40
Grande Albergo Ausonia
  & Hungaria, *Lido* 24

H

Harry's Bar, *San Marco* 44
Hotel Danieli, *San Marco* 20
Hotel Flora, *San Marco* 21
Hotel Metropole, *San Marco* 24

I

I Gesuiti, *Cannaregio* 116
I Muschieri, *San Marco* 57
I Rusteghi, *San Marco* 34
INPS Building, *Dorsoduro* 111
Isola della Certosa 122
Isola di San Giorgio Maggiore
  101, 115, 129
Israeli Pavilion, *Castello* 118

J

JW Marriott Venice Resort & Spa,
  Sacca Sessola 22 – 23

K

Kirikù, *San Marco* 49

L

La Bottega del Gusto, *Dorsoduro*
  38
La Cantina, *Cannaregio* 34
La Zucca, *San Polo* 37
L'Altra Ottica, *Castello and San
  Polo* 60
Law Courts, *Santa Croce* 105
Le Forcole, *Dorsoduro* 57

144

Le Stanze del Vetro, *San Giorgio Maggiore* 129
Legatoria Polliero, *San Polo* 54
Libreria Acqua Alta, *Castello* 61
Libreria Cluva, *Santa Croce* 61
Lido 24, 123, 129
Local, *Castello* 30
Locanda Cipriani, *Torcello* 129
Luca la Fenice, *Cannaregio* 124

M

Madera, *Dorsoduro* 53
Magazines 103
Marignana Arte, *Dorsoduro* 98
Marina e Susanna Sent, *Murano* 129
Massimo Micheluzzi, *Dorsoduro* 98
Mazzorbo 24, 127
Mercato del Carcere Femminile, *Giudecca* 33
Mercato di Rialto, *San Polo* 33
Micromega, *San Marco* 60
Millevini, *San Marco* 38
Murano 127, 129
Museo Correr, *San Marco* 93
Musica a Palazzo, *San Marco* 102

N

Need to know 14 – 15
Negozio Olivetti, *San Marco* 108 – 109
Noa di Nina, *San Marco* 49
Nordic Pavilion, *Castello* 118

O

Officine 904, *Dorsoduro* 58
Oh My Blue, *San Polo* 48
Ostaria Al Ponte, *Cannaregio* 34
Osteria alle Testiere, *Castello* 28
Osteria Anice Stellato, *Cannaregio* 37
Osteria Bancogiro, *San Polo* 27
Osteria Da Fiore, *San Polo* 28
Osteria Enoteca Ai Artisti, *Dorsoduro* 29
Ottica Urbani, *San Marco* 60
Ottico Fabbricatore, *San Marco* 50

P

Palazzo Fortuny, *San Marco* 89
Palazzo Franchetti, *San Marco* 36
Palazzo Grassi, *San Marco* 96
Palazzo Rio Novo, *Dorsoduro* 111
Palazzo Venart, *Santa Croce* 25
Palazzo Zenobio, *Dorsoduro* 114
Palwer, *San Marco* 59
Paradiso Perduto, *Cannaregio* 45
Pasticceria Dal Mas, *Cannaregio* 38
Pasticceria Rizzardini, *San Polo* 39

Pasticceria Tonolo, *Dorsoduro* 38
Piazza San Marco, *San Marco* 115
Piscina Sant'Alvise, *Cannaregio* 123
Ponte della Costituzione, *Santa Croce/Cannaregio* 104
Ponte di Rialto, *San Polo* 114
Punta della Dogana, *Dorsoduro* 94 – 95

Q

Quattro Fontane, *Lido* 24

R

Radio Ca' Foscari 103
Residenze a Mazzorbo, *Mazzorbo* 127
Resources 138 – 139
Ristorante Quadri, *San Marco* 29
Roberta di Camerino, *Cannaregio* 58
Rosa Salva, *San Marco* 38

S

Sacca Sessola 22 – 23, 124
Salviati, *Murano* 53
San Giorgio Maggiore, *Isola di San Giorgio Maggiore* 115, 129
San Marco 17, 20, 21, 24, 29, 34, 36, 38, 39, 41, 44, 47, 48, 49, 50, 51, 52, 57, 59, 60, 89, 93, 96, 97, 98, 99, 101, 102, 104, 108 – 109, 112, 114, 115, 124
San Michele 106
San Polo 18 – 19, 27, 28, 29, 31, 33, 35, 36, 37, 38, 39, 42, 48, 51, 54, 55, 59, 60, 90, 93, 114, 124
San Zaccaria, *Castello* 115
Santa Croce 16, 25, 33, 56, 61, 94, 104, 105, 106, 123
Santa Maria dei Derelitti, *Castello* 113
Santa Maria dei Miracoli, *Cannaregio* 117
Scala Contarini del Bovolo, *San Marco* 114
Scuola Grande di San Marco, *Castello* 114
Shirts & Ties, *San Marco* 47
Skyline Rooftop Bar, *Giudecca* 43
Stazione di Venezia Santa Lucia, *Cannaregio* 110

T

Teatrino di Palazzo Grassi, *San Marco* 101, 104
Teatro alle Tese, *Castello* 102
Teatro La Fenice, *San Marco* 101
Teatro Malibran, *Cannaregio* 102
Tessitura Luigi Bevilacqua, *Santa Croce* 56

Things we'd buy 62 – 64
Torcello 129
Torrefazione Cannaregio, *Cannaregio* 42
Trattoria al Gatto Nero, *Burano* 127
Trattoria al Ponte di Borgo, *Lido* 129
Tre Oci, *Giudecca* 93

U

Università Iuav di Venezia entrance, *Santa Croce* 106

V

Venice Kayak, *Isola della Certosa* 122
Venice Jazz Club, *Dorsoduro* 102
Venice Music Project, *Dorsoduro* 101
Venini, *Murano* 53, 127
Venissa, *Mazzorbo* 24, 127
Vinaria, *San Polo* 36
Vini da Gigio, *Cannaregio* 31
Vino Vero, *Cannaregio* 43
Vizio Virtù Cioccolateria, *Castello* 39
Voga alla Veneta, *Santa Croce* 123

Z

Zattere, *Dorsoduro* 125
Zuecca Project Space, *Giudecca* 90

Venice
Monocle Travel Series

New

Buy today at all good bookshops

You can also visit the online shops at *monocle.com* and *shop.gestalten.com* to get hold of your copies

The collection
We hope you have found the Monocle Travel Guide to Venice useful, inspiring and entertaining. There's plenty more to get your teeth into: we have a global suite of guides, with many more set to be released in the coming months. Cities are fun. Let's explore.

❶ London
The sights, sounds and style

❷ New York
Get a taste of the Big Apple's best

❸ Tokyo
The enigmatic glory of Japan's capital

❹ Hong Kong
Down to business in this vibrant city

❺ Madrid
Captivating capital abuzz with spirit

❻ Bangkok
Stimulate your senses with the exotic

❼ Istanbul
Thrilling fusion of Asia and Europe

❽ Miami
Unpack the Magic City's box of tricks

❾ Rio de Janeiro
Beaches, bars and bossa nova

❿ Paris
Be romanced by the City of Light

⓫ Singapore
Where modernity meets tradition

⓬ Vienna
Waltz through the Austrian capital

⓭ Sydney
Sun, surf and urban delights

⓮ Honolulu
Embrace Hawaii's aloha spirit

⓯ Copenhagen
Cycle through the Danish capital

⓰ Los Angeles
Fly high in the City of Angels

⓱ Toronto
Delve into this diverse Canadian city

⓲ Berlin
Discover the city of two halves

⓳ Rome
Scoot through the Eternal City

⓴ Venice
Wonder at the waterways

Maybe I do without clothes and keep the travel guides?